PAPUA NEW GUINEA

Making a Living

Teacher Resource Book

Pam Norman
Stephen Potek
Eron Hagunama
Joe Deruage

OXFORD
UNIVERSITY PRESS
AUSTRALIA & NEW ZEALAND

OXFORD
UNIVERSITY PRESS
AUSTRALIA & NEW ZEALAND

Level 8, 737 Bourke Street, Docklands, Victoria 3008, Australia

Oxford University Press is a department of the University of Oxford.
It furthers the University's objective of excellence in research,
scholarship, and education by publishing worldwide in

Oxford New York

Auckland Cape Town Dar es Salaam Hong Kong Karachi
Kuala Lumpur Madrid Melbourne Mexico City Nairobi
New Delhi Shanghai Taipei Toronto

With offices in

Argentina Austria Brazil Chile Czech Republic France Greece
Guatemala Hungary Italy Japan Poland Portugal Singapore
South Korea Switzerland Thailand Turkey Ukraine Vietnam

First published 2005
Reprinted 2006, 2007, 2008, 2009, 2010, 2013, 2014, 2020 (D), 2022 (D)

ISBN 978 0 19 555878 4

Designed and typeset by Lynn Twelftree
Printed and bound in Australia by Ligare Book Printers Pty Ltd

Acknowledgments
The Upper Primary Making a Living syllabus was prepared by the Curriculum Development Division of the Department of Education and was coordinated by Rachael Sivatevi Konaka.
The publishers would like to acknowledge the assistance of the Curriculum Development Division in the preparation of these resources, in particular John Kakas, Jennifer Sangga and Rachael Sivatevi Konaka.
These resources were developed with the support of the Australian Government through the Curriculum Reform Implementation Project and the publishers would like to acknowledge the assistance of Dr Graham Dawson, Barbara Hodgins and Mostyn Coleman.

Contents

Secretary's Message

Making a Living is a new subject area that aims to empower students with the essential life skills and knowledge to participate actively in society, to be self-reliant and to live sustainably now and in the future.

It combines the subjects of Commerce, Agriculture and Technology to promote useful and relevant life skills. It has been allocated 6 hours (360 minutes) per week to give teachers enough time to teach this very important subject.

Students will manage resources, promote better living and participate actively in community development. This subject depends on initiatives, dedication and commitment from teachers, students and the community. Its success will be evident through practical projects in the school and local community.

Making a Living is an important part of the reform curriculum that emphasises the need to teach our students to be enterprising and improve standards of living as called for in the Matane report: A Philosophy of Education for Papua New Guinea.

Students will investigate, create and design innovative ways of using available resources. They will make objects, cost them and evaluate the quality of their products and processes. This subject is relevant and useful for students leaving formal schooling after Grade 8 as well as those who will pursue studies in higher learning institutions.

Student Books 1 and 2, and the accompanying Teacher Resource Book, have been prepared to provide direct support for the achievement of syllabus outcomes. The content is consistent with, and promotes the teaching and learning models of, the syllabus and the related Department of Education Teachers Guide. These resources encompass a range of material including student activities, advice to teachers, assessment ideas, homework activities, project activities, reference information and a glossary of terms. They are intended to facilitate flexible learning activity for teachers and students, and may be modified and amended to suit local circumstances.

I commend and approve these materials for use in all Upper Primary schools throughout Papua New Guinea.

Peter M. Baki

Peter M. Baki CBE
Secretary for Education

Overview

Making a Living

'Making a Living' is a new subject that aims to provide students with learning experiences to acquire practical knowledge, skills, attitudes and values. These will assist students to become independent and creative in using local resources wisely to improve their quality of life. These skills should allow students to live productive lives in their communities once they have completed their schooling.

Much of the learning activity should take place through project work outside of the classroom. The subject has a generous time allocation of 360 minutes each week to allow for meaningful practical learning activities. The Making a Living process of 'investigate, plan and design, make or produce, market or use, evaluate' plays a central role in undertaking projects, particularly those of an income-generating nature. Students and teachers are encouraged to try new and interesting ideas to create new markets for their products.

Using the Student Books

Key features

The content of the student books is designed to be applicable to the diversity of learning contexts of students in Papua New Guinea. The success of implementing the Making a Living subject depends on student and teacher abilities to see opportunities in their local areas to use resources to plan personal or income-generating projects which benefit families and communities. Consequently, the content is flexible in that students in both urban and rural areas can relate to the information. Both the text and the illustrations reflect diverse contexts such as islands, highlands and mainland coastal environments.

The content of these books supports student learning for the Making a Living curriculum area. The books:

- directly support the new upper primary syllabus by following the sequence of strands and sub-strands, with one chapter or section for each strand and clearly identifiable topics for each sub-strand
- contain direct references to the new upper primary syllabus at the beginning of each chapter, demonstrating the clear relationship between the student book and the syllabus
- provide topics and learning approaches that directly support the achievement of syllabus outcomes. The subject content is based on the topics listed under 'Recommended Knowledge' subheadings in the section of the Making a Living Teacher Guide
- include a wide range of student activities at the end of each topic (which can be completed inside and outside the classroom), reference information and a glossary of terms. Most activities in the 'For You to Try' sections were derived from ideas under 'Recommended Skills and Suggested Activities' in the 'Elaborations' section of the Making a Living Teacher Guide
- use icons to indicate where book content has major links to other upper primary subjects

- are written at a reading level that is appropriate for upper primary students and with a format that allows teachers to use them in ways that best suit their objectives and personal teaching style
- draw extensively on examples that are culturally appropriate to upper primary students in Papua New Guinea, giving recognition and credibility to Papua New Guinean knowledge and customs
- use language that is gender sensitive and include positive gender roles
- use text as the main medium of the activity-based approach and include a good proportion of pictures and illustrations to support text
- require only those resources that are normally available to teachers in Papua New Guinea, especially those in rural and remote areas
- incorporate the Making a Living process of 'investigate, plan and design, make or produce, market or use, evaluate' into suggested activities for projects, particularly those of an income-generating nature

Using the Teacher Resource Book

Key features

The Teacher Resource Book, in conjunction with the Making a Living student books Book 1 and 2, will help teachers implement the Making a Living syllabus for upper primary students. It provides teachers with the following information:

- relevant information for planning a school-based program
- topics cross-referenced to other curriculum areas to allow for the development of integrated units of work
- a selection of teaching and learning strategies
- ideas for assessment activities
- topic elaborations to show how to develop topics covered in the student books into units of work
- how to extend and develop relevant content and contexts from the student books
- additional information that will assist teachers to develop their own units of work
- additional projects, investigations and activities to further extend students' skills

How to use it

When you receive this book you need to:

- read it carefully to get a sense of the information it contains and how it is organised
- read it carefully to become familiar with the strands and sub-strands, processes and skills, elaborations of learning outcomes and the teaching and learning strategies
- identify specific projects that your students could undertake based on the learning outcomes
- consider how to use the information to develop your own programs and units of work

Structure

The Teacher Resource Book is structured in the following way:

- Each chapter covers one syllabus strand from Making a Living (Strand 1: Managing Resources, Strand 2: Better Living, Strand 3: Community Development).
- At the beginning of each chapter there is an **overview page** which highlights:
  - ➢ the major outcomes of the strand and sub-strands
  - ➢ how these outcomes are developed over the three upper primary grade levels
  - ➢ key words and concepts used and developed throughout the chapter

- possible assessment tasks that could be carried out to assess students' knowledge and skills
- identified content that has major links to other upper primary subjects

- Two more sections are included in each chapter, namely:

  Teacher information—in this section added information is given to that already in the student book to enable teachers to develop units of work. A sample unit is also included at the end of some of these sections to show how a unit of work can be developed over a period of time to achieve specific outcomes.

  Class projects—a selection of projects that teachers may wish to develop depending on their suitability for the school's particular area as well as the availability of essential resources to undertake the proposed project.

- The **appendices** at the end of the book include:
  - all projects and investigations from the two student books
  - a complete glossary
  - sample forms
- **Icons**—there are icons throughout the student books. These icons indicate strong links to other subject areas. For example when dealing with preparing food, the icon will be the Personal Development icon to show that food and hygiene are connected.

  The icons look like this:

  ML MAL = Making a Living

  M M = Mathematics

  PD PD = Personal Development

  L L = Language

  A A = Arts

  S S = Science

  SS SS = Social Science

Learning Outcomes

Making a Living Teachers Guide states that:

'Learning outcomes describe specifically what students know and are able to do in each Strand and Grade. The outcomes are broad and can be achieved in any context depending on available resources and expertise.

The learning outcomes and indicators will:

- Give teachers the flexibility to write units of work and teaching programs suitable to local conditions, available resources and individual student needs.
- Guide teachers to select appropriate assessment tasks and assessment criteria.
- Help teachers plan and revise their future teaching programs.'

The content of *Making a Living* is organized into three strands and three sub-strands. Each sub-strand has a learning outcome, relating to a particular concept, and is developed across Grades 6, 7 and 8. Students are required to achieve 10 learning outcomes for each grade level as identified in the Making a Living Syllabus (pp. 11–13). Within each strand, students use processes and skills to achieve specific outcomes as summarized on page 4.

Strand	Concepts	Processes and Skills
Managing Resources Sub-strand: Land and water Sub-strand: The environment Sub-strand: Crop and animal management	Sustainability of resources Conservation and protection Food supply and security	These processes and skills apply to all strands: **Investigating** – gathering relevant information **Planning and designing** – transfer gathered information into an action plan **Making and Producing** – carrying out action plan **Marketing or using** – applying marketing strategies to sell products. If the product is not sold, how will it be used? **Evaluating** – make an informed judgment on the project and report findings
Better Living Sub-strand: Healthy living Sub-strand: Care and management Sub-strand: Wise consumer Sub-strand: Making things	Nutrition and hygiene Safety and management Money management Creativity and innovation	
Community Development Sub-strand: Knowing your communities Sub-strand: Communication Sub-strand: Community projects	Relationships Public relations Social and economic development	

Planning using outcomes

The Making a Living Teachers Guide includes Elaborations (pp. 12–36) which describe content (knowledge, skills and attitudes) and contexts (school environment, resources) that teachers can use to develop learning experiences and assessment. These Elaborations provide teachers with examples of what students need to know and do in order to achieve an outcome. Teachers need to use the Elaborations in the Teachers Guide to plan units of work to meet specific outcomes.

This sample class project shows how to match activities with process skills, and identify teaching strategies, assessment tasks and materials.

SAMPLE PROJECT UNIT: Caring for Clothes

Grade: 6
Strand: Better Living
Sub-strand: Healthy living
Learning outcome: *6.2.1 Describe and demonstrate aspects of personal hygiene, nutrition and safety that promote a healthy lifestyle.*
Purpose: The purpose of this unit is to allow students to learn and apply skills of mending, washing and ironing using their own clothes before developing a mending and laundering income-generating project for staff, students and the wider community.

UNIT CONTENT

Knowledge	Skills	Attitudes
Students demonstrate an understanding of: • mending, darning, patching, appliqué by hand and machine sewing • laundering processes (sorting, soaking, care skills, washing, rinsing, pegging, folding) • types of irons, ironing boards or ironing surfaces, heat needed for cotton or synthetic fabric	Students develop the skills to: • mend clothes • use sewing equipment appropriately • wash clothes • peg to retain shape of clothes • use irons safely and appropriately • iron different types of clothes • fold clothes neatly • market their skills to develop an income generating project	Students develop attitudes: • the value of caring for clothes to prolong usefulness and attractiveness • the economic value of having clothes • appreciation of skills for life • pride in achievement

Overview of teaching and learning activities

Process skills	Teaching and learning strategies		Materials
Investigation	• explore common causes of damage to clothes • analyse how clothes are constructed • conduct a market survey of needs for a clothes care service	interview family members demonstration excursion	student clothes from home questionnaire
Planning and designing	• choose appropriate resources to mend, wash and iron clothes • identify options and constraints • plan activities in a logical sequence and develop action plans	discussion creative thinking problem-solving flow chart	chart paper writing materials
Making or producing	• develop skills using own clothes • apply appropriate techniques • use equipment safely • produce results of high quality • manage time and resources effectively	modelling supervised practice	sewing and laundering equipment and facilities
Marketing or using	• decide affordable prices for a range of services and clothing types • advertise service to a targeted audience • keep records • determine profit	discussion group work brainstorming creative thinking	materials for making displaying advertisements
Evaluation	• identify successes, failures and constraints • determine whether the project met the intended outcome • suggest adaptations to improve • analyse the viability of the project	reflection journal writing	writing materials

Assessment plan

Method	Task	Criteria	Recording
Observation of student work	Darning	• cut fabric piece to go under damaged area • neat stitching sewn over damaged area • neat finish; clothing item is now repaired and serviceable	checklist
Observation of student work	Laundering	• water collected in suitable container • dirty areas rubbed with soap • clothes rinsed • clothes wrung to remove excess water • clothes hung or spread to dry • clothes folded neatly when dry	checklist

Planning

Planning, programming, assessing and reporting involve the consideration of the individual learning needs of all students and the creation of a learning environment that assists students to achieve the outcomes of the syllabus. Students' achievement of the syllabus outcomes is the goal of planning, programming and assessing. The sequence of learning experiences that teachers provide should build on what students already know and should be designed to ensure that they progress through the levels identified in the syllabus. However, it is not intended that all activities will be assessed.

All lessons should be planned so that outcomes, assessment and classroom practice are all integrated. Assessment should not be tagged onto the end of a section of work but should be planned at the same time as planning the lesson content and should be ongoing.

Teaching programs need to be developed by teachers to structure learning experiences over a period of time. These programs should consist of:

A long-term plan—such as a yearly or two-year plan—where teachers identify units of work that will be implemented over a long period of time. Teachers decide on the duration of these units of work in their long-term plan.

Short-term plans—These require the teacher to develop the units of work identified in the long-term plan. These units of work are generally planned to be implemented within one term. Most integrated units of work should only take about 2–4 weeks, so teachers will need to plan several units of work for each term.

Lesson plans—These are generally a further breakdown of the short-term plan (that is, the type of lessons that will be undertaken to achieve the short-term plan's objectives).

Assessment

Assessment should be an integral part of the teaching and learning process and focus on how well students achieve the learning outcomes. Most teaching involves assessment, and by planning what to assess and recording the specific assessment information, appropriate assessment data can be collected.

There are a number of purposes for assessment:

- to collect and analyse information about students' competencies
- to provide guidance, feedback and information about students' achievements and progress to students and parents
- to inform program decision-making and classroom organisational techniques

The most important purpose of assessment is to improve student learning. Assessment stems naturally from the teaching/learning situation. Teachers in their interaction with children constantly assess:

- students' current understandings
- the nature of any misconceptions
- students' current needs

Assessing and teaching cannot be separated, and assessment should inform teaching. Assessment is about finding out what children know and can do. The teacher constantly needs to ask:

- What do I want to know?
- How will I find out?

This should be an ongoing process as:

- assessing learners continuously enables teachers to closely monitor and understand their progress
- ongoing formal continuous assessment helps teachers diagnose problem areas in both learning and teaching, and allows teachers to adjust their teaching accordingly
- learners receive helpful feedback after every assessment

Strategies

Assessment strategies selected by the teacher should be appropriate to the situation and to the purpose of the assessment. Teachers have the opportunity to observe and record aspects of students' learning in a range of situations.

Group work—The teacher can determine the extent of student interaction and participation.

Listening—Listening to students respond to questions as well as other input, the teacher can collect many clues about students' current understanding and attitudes.

Interviewing students—Teachers can collect specific information about the way in which students think about certain situations.

Other sources of information for assessment purposes include the following:

- samples of students' work
- oral explanations or demonstrations to others
- questions posed by students
- practical tasks
- investigations and/or projects
- students' oral and written reports
- short quizzes
- pen and paper test

STRAND 1 Managing Resources

About this strand

In the Managing Resources strand, students learn that people depend on the environment for food, water, shelter and clean air. They understand and value natural resources and learn ways of managing land and water resources in sustainable ways that benefit people and the environment. Students learn principles and techniques of managing land to increase the quality and quantity of food production for their own consumption and for sale. There is a clear focus upon concepts of ecological and economic sustainability. They undertake environmentally friendly activities to protect and conserve the environment.

The Making a Living process of 'investigate, plan or design, make or produce, market or use, evaluate' should underpin the planning of learning activities. Students will consider new and interesting ways to use resources. It is expected that much of the learning and application of learning will occur out of the classroom in observation, investigation and practical activities. This should be reflected in assessment processes.

The three sub-strands of the Managing Resources strand are:

- land and water
- environment
- crops and animal management

There is one learning outcome for each sub-strand for each grade. The learning outcomes are broad and can be achieved in any context depending on available resources and expertise. Elaborating on the learning outcomes generates ideas that help the teacher to identify content and activities, possible projects and assessment tasks. From the learning outcome elaborations, teachers can write units of work and teaching programs relevant to the community served by the school.

The following is a sample elaboration of the Grade 6 learning outcome. The ideas are not exhaustive and teachers are encouraged to develop their own.

Example of elaborating a learning outcome

Grade: 6

Strand: Managing Resources

Sub-strand: Land and water

Learning outcome: *6.1.1 Students investigate the importance of land and water resources and apply appropriate ways of managing these to meet basic human needs.*

Four key areas can be derived from this outcome: land resources, water resources, managing these resources and human needs. Each area can be elaborated.

For example, the area of water resources can be elaborated as follows:

- Identify the main features of water resources in specific areas such as rivers, creeks, lakes, swamps, ocean. For example, a creek generally is shallow and not very wide; people can walk across. Most creeks have flowing water that can be used for water supply to a village. Creeks can be polluted because they are used by many people and the water may be unclean. Other creeks, such as those in the highlands, are very fast flowing and deep, so people need to consider safety when using these creeks.
- Discover how water resources are used by the local community to meet their needs. For example:
  - ➢ transport—this can be further extended by looking at the types of water transport people build (such as canoes) or use (such as motor canoes, small boats powered by diesel)
  - ➢ food supply—what type of foods can be sourced from the water and their nutritional value in ensuring a balanced diet
  - ➢ water supply for house and garden—types of water collecting systems installed by people to get water to their houses
  - ➢ ceremonies associated with water—collection of shells and other objects that are used in ceremonies
  - ➢ leisure activities such as swimming, canoeing
- Investigate the types of water life that can be found. Identify types of marine life in rivers, creeks, lakes, swamps and the ocean; how they are caught; what uses beside supplying food they can be put to, such as providing crocodile skins or shells for artefacts, jewellery and shell money.

From the ideas generated, the teacher can decide on appropriate topics to include in a unit of work, taking into account students' prior knowledge, water resources in the locality and expertise available. The elaboration provides ideas of topics to investigate and activities for students to do.

The *time allocation* for Making a Living is 360 minutes per week. This allows the teacher to plan activities that require perhaps half a day outside the classroom. On water resources, for example:

Monday	Tuesday	Wednesday	Thursday	Friday
1pm–3pm Plan outing, what to look for, questions to ask. Walk around and observe how water is being used or misused; ask questions, collect and record information.		1pm–3pm Discuss and plan ways of improving management of water resources Implement a strategy, e.g. clean waterways, fix dripping taps, build a drain or soak pit	1pm–3pm Consider ways to evaluate the work done. Develop criteria. Revisit work sites. Evaluate sustainability of work done. Consider continuation or other water projects.	

Assessment is an ongoing process and should be carried out as students undertake activities. Possible assessment ideas for the above example may include:

- plan five questions to ask on how water is used to meet human needs
- record observations of how water is used and misused
- analyse a water related problem and how practices may affect the water ecological system
- develop and implement an action plan to address a problem with a water resource
- evaluate benefit of project as an effective water management strategy

SUB-STRAND 1 Land and water

Main ideas

The main idea of the 'land and water' sub-strand is for students to gain knowledge about the importance of land and water resources to meet basic human needs. Land resources are all the resources found on land such as plants, animals, minerals and soil. Water resources are all the resources found in the oceans, rivers, creeks and lakes. Students will learn ways of using these resources and at the same time not damaging the environment.

The learning outcomes for each upper primary grade for this sub-strand are shown in the following table:

Grade 6	Grade 7	Grade 8
6.1.1 Students investigate the importance of land and water resources and apply appropriate ways of managing these to meet basic human needs.	7.1.1 Students investigate and compare consequences of mismanagement of land and water resources and plan, design and undertake a small project using appropriate management practices.	8.1.1 Students evaluate current practices of land and water resource management to design sustainable resource managements projects to generate income.

Key words

land resources, water resources, human needs, conservation, sustainable management, biodiversity, exploitation, pollution, ecosystem, recycling, subsistence farming, commercial farming, permaculture, organic farming

Possible assessment tasks

Assessment aims to gather information on how well students achieve the learning outcomes for Sub-strand 1 (Land and water). Assessment should encourage improved normal practices, and innovative and interesting entrepreneurial practices. Clear criteria should be set for satisfactory completion of tasks.

The suggested activities are organised from simple school- or home-based activities (Grade 6 level) to more complex community-based ones (Grade 8 level); however, these levels are not prescriptive and teachers should choose activities according to students' needs and abilities.

Land and water activities suitable for developing into assessment tasks include:

1. make plant pots from recycled materials
2. grow flowers
3. make wreaths and flower leis
4. replace washers on leaking taps
5. repair gutters and damaged water pipes
6. establish a cold-water drinking service
7. keep water supplies pollution free
8. collect rubbish from beaches and rivers
9. conduct a water-sports day

10 race canoes

11 make water fountains

12 build soak pits or drains

13 dig a new well, put in new pipes

14 construct attractive recreation areas beside water features

15 build sea walls

16 establish a nursery

17 plan canoe or river excursions as a tourist activity

18 sell cut flowers and flower arrangements

19 sell plant cuttings and potted plants

20 sell dried or pressed flowers

21 plant trees for:
– reforestation
– firewood supplies
– shade
– fruit or nut produce.

Major links to other subjects

'Land and water' builds upon student learning in lower primary subjects, in particular Environmental Studies and Community Living. At the upper primary level, 'land and water' has major links to the 'living things' strand of Science and the 'people and environment' sub-strand of Social Science. These links are noted as icons in the student books (see page 3 for a list of icons).

Teacher information

Land resources

Land resources include minerals, crops, animals and forests. Minerals are significant land resources. They provide valuable income for the government, landowners and employees. The income is used to meet human needs in the services the government can provide and for personal use by individuals.

Crops, animals and forests meet our physical needs for food, clothing and building material. They can be sold in different forms and provide us with a monetary income. Feathers, skins, flowers and leaves are used in traditional dress and for other decorative purposes. The relationship between plants, animals and the natural environment can be maintained through good management practices.

Food crops

The main starchy food eaten by an individual or family is called its 'staple' food. Staple crops in Papua New Guinea include bananas, cassava, corn, potato, rice, sago, sweet potato, different types of taro and yam.

Legume crops are significant as an important source of vegetable protein. They are particularly valuable where families do not have a regular supply of animal protein. Legume crops include peas, mung beans, peanuts, snake beans, soya beans and winged beans.

Traditional green leafy vegetables called *kumu* are important sources of vitamins and minerals in a person's diet. These include aibika, aupa, ferns, kangkong, taro leaves and pumpkin tips. There are many local names. Other common coloured vegetables include cabbage, lettuce, tomatoes, capsicum, spring onions, leeks, pumpkin, choko, eggplant, broccoli, cauliflower and carrots.

A wide variety of fruits and nuts are found throughout Papua New Guinea and are important sources of vitamins and minerals in a person's diet. These include avocado, breadfruit, citrus fruit, coconut, custard apple, durian, galip nut, granadilla, guava, jackfruit, macadamia nut, mango, mangosteen, passionfruit, pawpaw, pineapple, rambutan and soursop. Sugar cane is another important food source.

Cash crops

Cash crops ranked by value are coffee, oil palm, cocoa, copra, tea, rubber and sugar. Vanilla has grown in importance in recent times. The crops are grown by individuals and companies. Growers sell their products to factories or exporters in return for cash. Many people make a living from growing cash crops.

Animals

Animal resources for humans include pigs, chickens, ducks, pigeons, cassowaries, cuscus, wallabies, bandicoots, bats, snakes, crocodiles, Birds of Paradise, beef cattle, goats, dogs, water buffalo and horses. Animal resources meet human needs in different ways. Horses provide a means of transport. Water buffalo pull carts. Dogs are used for hunting or kept as pets for company. Feathers from birds are used in headdresses. Snake skins are used on drums. Crocodile skins are exported. Pigs may be used as part of bride price or compensation ceremonies. Chickens and eggs are important sources of protein food. Many people make a living from raising animals for personal use or to generate an income.

Forests

Forests are an important source of timber for housing, boat building, firewood and logging. Forest plantations have been established in various parts of the country such as the pine forests at Bulolo-Wau, teak forests at Brown River and Kerema, and others in the Gogol valley, Kimbe and in the Highlands. The country has extensive forest reserves, which cover three-quarters of its land surface. Papua New Guinea produces considerable quantities of timber. Plywood and wood chip production and milling are of some importance.

Minerals

Minerals are another valuable land resource. Government revenues and foreign exchange earning depend heavily on mineral exports. Indigenous landowners in areas affected by mineral projects also receive royalties from those operations. Papua New Guinea is richly endowed with gold, copper, nickel and other minerals as well as oil and natural gas. Copper and gold mines are currently in production at Porgera, Ok Tedi, Misima, and Lihir. New nickel, copper and gold projects have been identified and are waiting to begin development. A consortium led by Chevron is producing and exporting oil from the Southern Highlands Province. Plans have been drawn up to build a gas pipeline from Papua New Guinea to Queensland and get benefits from the country's estimated 22.5 trillion cubic feet of natural gas reserves.

Water resources

Water resources come from rain, dams, tanks, wells, oceans, rivers, coral reefs, lakes, mangroves, wetlands and swamps. People need a water supply for drinking, cooking, washing and flushing toilets. Although Papua New Guinea has an abundance of water resources, 70 per cent of the rural population has no access to safe water, and sanitation is a major problem. Furthermore, many people travel long distances to collect water.

One method of making water safe for human consumption is by boiling it and letting it cool. The water should be boiled at a rolling boil for five minutes before removing it from the heat source. Another method which kills harmful bacteria is by adding chlorine to water supplies.

Dirty water can also be made less dirty by sedimentation and filtration. In the sedimentation method, water is let stand for the coarser particles to settle to the bottom. In the filtration method, water runs through sand or a fine cloth that catches the coarser particles. In both these cases, the water should still be boiled or chlorinated to be safe to drink.

A good quality, conveniently located source of water is important for people's health. Diseases such as diarrhoea, typhoid and dysentery are caused by poor quality drinking water.

Food from water sources includes fish, trout, tuna, sharks, crabs, prawns, crayfish, shell-food, oysters and turtles. Much of the country's freshwater and marine fishing is of a subsistence nature, but there is some commercial fishing, especially for prawns, crayfish and tuna. Fishing licences sold to foreign fishing fleets are also an important revenue source. Sustainable practices are currently being implemented to ensure seafood supplies for future generations.

Sea-shells may be sold, used as money or used to make necklaces, armbands and other decorative purposes.

Human needs

Human needs include air, food, water, shelter, clothes, love, protection and safety. In our modern cash society, people also need money to enrich the quality of their lives by buying things they cannot provide themselves.

The importance of resources

Resources are important for physiological, monetary, aesthetic and ecological purposes.

Physiology refers to the body, so physiological resources are things we need for a healthy body. Air, water and food, along with the materials we use for clothing and shelter, are examples of physiological resources. They are important for human health and survival.

Monetary resources

Monetary resources are things we can sell, or can make into something to sell, in order to get a money income. The knowledge and skills of people are resources. All the nation's land and water resources are important if they are utilised to benefit the economic status of the people. We value land and water resources that enable us to earn money and provide a means of livelihood to pay for the things we need and want.

Aesthetic resources

Aesthetic resources are artistic things we use to beautify the environment, our homes and ourselves. We put curtains in our houses, flowers in our hair, pictures on our walls, gardens around our houses and designs on our clothes for aesthetic purposes. The resources we use are important to provide us with a pleasant and attractive appearance and environment.

Ecology refers to the relationship of plants and animals to their physical and biological environment. It is important to use resources in a sustainable way so that they remain useful for future generations. Reusing, reducing and recycling waste products are important practices for ecological purposes. Controlling mining, forestry and fishing industries is another important way of ensuring that the ecology of an environment is not destroyed. Each of us needs to use environmentally friendly practices.

Sustainable resource management

Sustainable resource management is the planned practice of using things in a way that will keep them going for the future generations. Sustainable resource management practices include permaculture, mixed cropping, reusing resources, conserving resources, sharing resources, protecting marine areas and organic farming.

Permaculture

Permaculture (permanent agriculture) is a system of agriculture that does not involve yearly crops but uses crops that are self-sustaining (for example, sweet potato, taro, yam, sugar cane, bananas, coconuts, corn). Another definition of permaculture is the harmonious integration of landscape and people, providing their food, fuel, shelter and other material needs in a sustainable way. Traditional subsistence farming methods in Papua New Guinea could be considered examples of permaculture. Cuttings, seeds or suckers from plants ensured that varieties of crops were sustained from one generation to the next.

Mixed cropping

Mixed cropping is where varieties of crops are grown in the food gardens, plantations and forests. The benefit is that different crops take and replace different nutrients in the soil. Some with shallow roots and others with deeper roots take and replace nutrients at various levels in the soils. Some crops also minimise damage by pests to other plants.

Reusing resources

An example of reusing resources is the use of mulch and compost. A thick layer of mulch on the soil surface stops weeds from growing and helps to retain the moisture content of the soil. After it disintegrates, it can be mixed into the soil. Compost is made from a mixture of plant matter and animal manure. This is dug into the soil when garden beds are being prepared to enrich the soil nutrient content.

Conserving resources

Conserving resources is important for sustainability. Conservation refers to the sustainable use and protection of natural resources including plants, animals, mineral deposits, soils, clean water, clean air and fossil fuels (such as coal, petroleum and natural gas). Natural resources are grouped into two categories, renewable and non-renewable. A *renewable* resource is one that may be replaced over time by natural processes, such as fish populations or natural vegetation, or one that cannot be used up, such as solar energy. The goal of conserving renewable resources is to ensure that such resources are not consumed faster than they are replaced. *Non-renewable* resources are those in limited supply that cannot be replaced or can be replaced only over extremely long periods of time. These include mineral deposits, soils, coal, petroleum and natural gas.

Sharing resources avoids wastage. If two people travelled in one boat or vehicle instead of each person travelling alone, the effort and fuel use would be halved. If several families made one big mumu instead of each making their own, again the effort and fuel use would be lessened. If a village had one set of tools or equipment that could be shared, this would lessen the resources needed to equip each family. Where practicable, sharing resources is an example of a sustainable practice.

Organic farming

Organic farming promotes the use of natural materials and farming methods. Traditional subsistence farming reflects organic farming methods and is sustainable. Organic farming does not use chemicals and fertilisers.

There are many appropriate ways of managing resources for sustainability. Protecting wildlife areas and coral reefs ensures the survival of endangered species. Using sustainable fishing, gathering and hunting practices avoids waste of life and ensures survival for the future. Reusing and recycling resources reduces the energy and materials needed for further production. Tyres, glass, scrap metal, timber off-cuts, old furniture, clothes that have been outgrown, paper, aluminium and motor oil can all be recycled. Drainage and contour gardening helps to prevent soil erosion. Rotating crops, mulching and composting improve soil quality. Controlling numbers of grazing animals and the area where they graze can protect vegetation. Eliminating the pollution of waterways maintains the cleanliness and safe use of water. Revegetation and reforestation ensures growth of plants and trees for future use. Repairing leaking taps and tanks promptly saves water wastage.

Mismanagement practices

Mismanagement practices reduce the availability of resources. **Logging** areas without a reforestation program causes loss of plant diversity, animal habitats and soils. **Continuous cropping** on the same piece of land depletes the fertility of the soil, which then requires much time to recover and the use of fertilisers. Low production of food also occurs over time. **Dynamite fishing** is dangerous, destroys reefs and causes unnecessary killing of fish. Lack of reducing, reusing and recycling habits causes huge amounts of waste products, and also means that additional materials and energy are needed to produce new consumer products. **Pollution** of oceans and waterways kills fish and makes water unfit for human consumption.

Class projects

Choose projects from the list below that are appropriate for the school's local area and available resources. Set clear criteria for the satisfactory completion of tasks.

1 Establish a plant nursery. Investigate what plants people would be prepared to buy. Grow plants that could be sold as plant cuttings, pot plants or cut-flowers.

2 Establish a vegetable garden. Plan garden beds with drains and contouring to prevent soil erosion. Mix compost with the soil. Use mixed cropping or crop rotation strategies. Mulch gardens when plants begin to grow. Use water thoughtfully.

3 Plan and implement a recycling or reusing project. Investigate waste products in the locality that are suitable to reuse or recycle. The project could be to make a drum oven, flower vase or fence.

4 Improve the community water supply—for example, dig a new well, put in new piping, collect rubbish from beaches and rivers, fix leaking taps or build drains and soak pits.

5 Plant fruit or shade trees. Choose suitable locations. Prepare the ground well. Build a low protection fence to guard them from damage. Provide appropriate care.

This sample class project shows how to match activities with process skills, and identify teaching strategies, assessment tasks and materials.

SAMPLE CLASS PROJECT: Mixed Crop Project

Grade: 6
Strand: Managing Resources
Sub-strand: Land and water
Learning outcome: *6.1.1 Students investigate the importance of land and water resources and apply appropriate ways of managing these to meet basic human needs.*

Overview of teaching and learning activities

Process skills	Learning and teaching activities		Assessment tasks	Materials
Investigation	• visit a vegetable farm project • research and gather information about the mixed crop project • identify suitable sites for growing the mixed crops	excursion invite a guest speaker from your school community talk to the class about good gardening skills		
Planning and designing	• list activities needed for growing mixed cropping • identify resources and where to obtain them • calculate/estimate cost and expected income • prepare a garden diary	group work • clearing • measuring • digging • composting • mulching		

Process skills	Learning and teaching activities		Assessment tasks	Materials
Making or producing	• clear the land and prepare the soil • construct the nursery • construct a compost shed • plant vegetable seeds in nursery • transplant the seedlings • observe and keep records of the growth stages from planting to harvesting • apply fertiliser and insecticides • harvest the produce and take to the market	demonstration or arrange a visit to a model farm	nursery preparation transplanting seedlings	grass knives bush knives packets of seeds spades forks nylon ropes wheelbarrow
Evaluation	• identify problems encountered in growing mixed vegetables in an area and make suggestions for future improvements • analyse crop records	discussion		write a brief report about the success of the project

SUB-STRAND 2 The environment

Main ideas

The main ideas of the 'environment' sub-strand are to allow students to learn about the environment in which they live and apply appropriate practices to conserve and protect the environment. This includes the natural, built and social environments. Students learn about the elements of the local environment, consequences when an element is affected, causes and effects of waste and rubbish products, types of waste items, ecological values, economical values and cultural values. They undertake environmentally friendly actions to protect and conserve the environment.

The learning outcomes for each upper primary grade for this sub-strand are shown in the following table:

Grade 6	Grade 7	Grade 8
6.1.2 Students investigate the consequences when an element of the local environment is affected and suggest possible environmentally friendly actions to care for it.	7.1.2 Students investigate and undertake practical ways to reduce, reuse and recycle waste to benefit and improve the local environment.	8.1.2 Students describe and reflect on economical, cultural and ecological values of natural, social and built resources and apply environmentally friendly ways of managing the environment.

Key words

environment, consequences, reducing, recycling, reusing, ecology, reforestation, conservation, protection, pollution, habitats, natural environment, built environment

Possible assessment tasks

Assessment aims to gather information on how well students achieve the learning outcomes for Sub-strand 2 (The environment). Clear criteria should be set for satisfactory completion of tasks.

The suggested activities are organised from simple school- or home-based activities (Grade 6 level) to more complex community-based ones (Grade 8 level); however, these levels are not prescriptive and teachers should choose activities according to students' needs and abilities.

Environment activities suitable for developing into assessment tasks include:

1. collect materials for recycling: recycle products to make wrapping paper, hats, floor rugs, drum ovens, flower vases, fences, protective screens for young trees
2. landscape, cut long grass, remove weeds, trim trees, rake grounds, pick up plastic bags and other waste products
3. improve waste-disposal practices, paint rubbish bins, build rubbish-bin stands, build an incinerator, put up signs for a clean environment
4. create a mini-botanical garden or rainforest, establish protected areas
5. demonstrate soil-conservation practices, such as creating lawns or cut-grass areas, growing legumes, crop rotation, composting, contouring and mulching
6. offer services for garden care, tree-trimming or lawn-mowing
7. plan an ecotourism project: bush walks; river rides; tour guiding, including guided tours of local plants and land features; diving expeditions; wildlife adventures.

Major links to other subjects

Studies of the environment build upon student learning in lower primary subjects, in particular Environmental Studies and Community Living. At the upper primary level, 'environment' has major links to the 'living things' strand of Science and the 'people and environment' strand of Social Science. These links are noted as icons in the student books.

Teacher information

Our environment is the world around us. It consists of natural elements, things made by humans and human interactions with each other. We can consider our environment as consisting of natural, built and social elements. These elements connect in many ways. These parts are interacting and interdependent. They should not be seen as separate or competing. The quality of the interrelationships defines the health and well being of the total environment. There are consequences when an element is affected, whether it is by natural or human causes. The condition of the environment ultimately determines the quality and survival of life.

Today we recognise the need to be aware of the impact of our actions on the environment. We need to be aware of positive actions we can take to preserve and manage the environment for the future. Changes to the world's natural systems are occurring rapidly. The changes in weather patterns, climate and sea levels are complex. Human survival will depend on improved understanding at a global level and appropriate action to ensure the diversity and stability of life on earth. 'Think globally, act locally' is an appropriate slogan.

Consider the elements of healthy and unhealthy environments. A healthy environment has clean air, safe clean water for drinking and cooking, food for the family's needs, physically fit people, good houses, fertile soil, attractive physical surroundings, sound waste management practices, no obvious signs of pollution and friendly relationships amongst the people.

An unhealthy environment has smoky air, polluted water for drinking and cooking, infertile soil, poor crops, sick or weak people, dirty houses, unattractive physical surroundings, poor waste management practices, litter, graffiti, betel nut spit, and arguments and distrust amongst the people.

Elements of the natural environment

Our natural environment is composed of hills, mountains, valleys, rivers, oceans and lakes, with millions of life forms in plants, trees, fish, mammals, insects, spiders, amphibians, crustaceans, birds and reptiles. Important elements of our natural environment are:

- the producers (green plants)
- the consumers (herbivores and carnivores)
- the decomposers (fungi and bacteria)
- the nonliving components (dead organic matter and nutrients in the soil and water)

Ecology is the study of plants and animals in relation to their surroundings. Many interactions between living things are the result of the need for living things to feed. For example, plants absorb nutrients from their non-living surroundings that they then use to make food by the process of photosynthesis. Hence they are known as producers. Plants may then in turn be eaten by herbivores (animals who depend on plants for their own food), which in turn can be eaten by carnivores (animals who eat other animals for food). These are known as consumers. Humans are omnivores, eating both plants and animals.

The natural elements of the environment include sun, air, water, earth, the physical cycles that support life (oxygen, nitrogen, carbon and water) and biological and ecological systems (living things and their interrelationships). The air is a mixture of gases that living things rely on to survive. Humans and animals breathe in oxygen and breathe out carbon dioxide. Plants do the opposite. Plants take in carbon dioxide and give off oxygen. This relationship between plants, humans and animals is vital for survival. Destruction of vast areas of rain forest reduces the amount of oxygen going into the air.

What are the elements of your local natural environment? How are they used and affected by human activity?

Elements of the built environment

People interact with the natural environment and convert it into a human habitat by arranging and changing their surroundings to suit their needs and wants. In remote rural areas, we see land being cleared for houses and gardens. There are walking tracks that disturb the natural environment. Natural resources are used for housing, canoes, clothing and tools.

Today, with rapidly advancing technology, humans have greater powers to change the natural environment. Humans have radically changed the appearance of the natural environment. The effects are readily seen in towns. There are roads, houses, churches, schools, hospitals, shops, markets, electricity power poles, vehicles, drains and rubbish. The effects are also seen in rural areas where large tracts of natural landscape have been transformed by plantations, cattle stations, forestry projects and mines. Human activity has a huge impact on the natural environment. Often, we have failed to realise the consequences of our actions.

What are the elements of your local built environment? What impact do they have on the natural environment?

Social elements of the environment

A person does not live in isolation. Humans are social animals and survive in communities that are characterised by friendly companionship and relationships. Evidence of social elements is seen in family groups, *wantok* system, villages, sporting teams, church groups, schools and clans. People in social groups share common interests and meet their needs in similar ways.

These social groupings are important. From them people obtain a sense of belonging and establish cultural values. These values are reflected in their codes of acceptable behaviour, use of technology, the institutions they establish, modes of government, economic activities, settlement patterns, religious observances and things they value for aesthetic purposes.

What are the distinctive features of the social environment in your locality? What problems exist and how are these social problems counteracted?

Consequences for the environment

Consequences are the effects or results of something that has happened previously. There is a cause and effect relationship. Some examples are as follows:

- Heavy rain washes away top soil from gardens.
- A volcanic eruption or tidal wave destroys a town or community.
- A landslide damages a road and people cannot transport goods to market.
- Forestry projects cause a loss of habitat for animals.
- Over-use of chemical sprays and fertilisers can pollute water supplies.
- Polluted water and unhygienic conditions cause outbreaks of diarrhoea, dysentery or typhoid.
- Overgrazing of animals destroys vegetation cover and productive soils.

In 2004, heavy flooding washed away two bridges on the road from Madang to Lae. A large section of the Monia bridge fell into the Homia river making it impassable. Transport between Lae and Madang was disrupted. Two power pylons collapsed. This disrupted the electricity supply from the Ramu-Yonki power grid to Madang. The old generators in Madang had to be brought into use to supply the town. They did not have sufficient capacity to supply all the town at once, and there was load shedding. Many shops and institutions relied on their own back-up generators for power until the problem was fixed. Fuel supplies ran low because of the extra, unexpected demand. This is an example of the consequences when an element of the environment is affected.

Soil erosion and soil loss are a consequence of human activity. Chopping down trees, clearing forests, logging, overgrazing, over-cultivation, mining, construction of buildings, transport and building pylons for electricity cables are all examples of human activity that affects the soil layer in different ways and causes soil loss.

The consequences of mining activities affect natural, built and social environments. Mining directly disturbs the land in reshaping its surface with pits and roads. Mines destroy natural habitats. Buildings and large processing plants are built. Social environments are changed as landowners and mining employees develop relationships.

The consequences of environmental pollution

affect the land, air and water. Exhaust fumes from vehicles and aircraft, smoke and gases from factories pollute the air we breathe. This can cause bronchitis, pneumonia and associated respiratory complaints. Waste products such as paper, plastic bags and household waste pollute the land. They are ugly to look at and attract vermin that can cause health problems. Chemicals and sewage pollute our waterways and can cause health problems.

It is becoming evident that as more and more bush is cleared, there is a danger that many species of animals, insects and wildlife will become extinct. Some introduced species of animals and insects invade local ecosystems and destroy plants and other animal species. The coffee rust, a fungal disease, damages coffee leaves and can destroy young coffee trees. Cattle breeders must be on the lookout for any outbreak of food and mouth disease. This must be reported to agricultural officers so that the disease does not spread to other parts of the country.

The call now is for people to be aware of ways in which we damage our environment and to take the necessary action to conserve and protect our resources for the future survival of our planet and all that lives on it.

Types of waste and rubbish products

What would you find in a rubbish bin? There could be food scraps, vegetable peelings, sugar cane waste, garden clippings, coconuts, fluorescent light tubes, paper, glass bottles, tins, cardboard packaging, rags, plastic bags, plastic wrappers off biscuits or ice blocks, fish and animal bones and prawn shells.

What would you find in a community rubbish dump? There could be old stoves, refrigerators, lamps, washing machines, vehicles, bikes, tyres, furniture, pipes, scrap metal, paint tins, car batteries and all the usual household waste.

Bodily waste includes urine and faeces from humans and animals. These need to be disposed of in hygienic, environmentally friendly ways. Animal wastes can be used as added fertiliser for soils and mixed with plant cuttings in compost heaps. They should not be left on the ground where people may walk. Human waste should not fall on the ground where people walk as this can lead to hookworm infections. Pit, pan and septic toilets are acceptable receptacles for human waste.

An investigation could be conducted into waste products from families, stores and businesses in the locality. Waste management practices can be evaluated and better methods suggested.

Environmentally friendly waste management practices

A community needs to have environmentally friendly waste management practices. One approach is follow the three R's—recycle, reduce and reuse. Instead of throwing things away and adding to the problem of waste pollution, we should think of ways to recycle, reduce or reuse products. We can have a major impact on the amount of rubbish we produce by becoming aware of how much we throw out and changing some of our habits about buying and using things. The waste we create has to be carefully controlled to be sure that it does not harm our environment and our health.

To **recycle** is to change a resource to make another useful product. Old clothes, furniture, tyres, paper, cardboard, plastic, pipes, glass and aluminium are examples of materials that can be recycled. Children's clothes can be made from an old laplap or bed sheet. Wood from a damaged table could be turned into a stool. A plastic drink bottle can be turned into a plant holder. Scrap sheet metal can be made into a barbecue plate or cooking tray. Cardboard cartons can be made into storage boxes. Coconut shells can be turned into bowls, buttons or necklaces. Rice and flour bags can be made into carry bags. Paint tins can be recycled as sawdust stoves. Small fuel drums can be turned into seats with a cushion on top.

To **reduce** means to make something smaller or to use less. Buy and use less of everything. Use bilums instead of plastic bags when shopping.

When you have a choice, buy plain packaged products instead of ones with flashy bulky packaging. Buying a large-sized product instead of two or more smaller products reduces waste and packaging materials. Start a compost heap to reduce the amount of food or garden scraps being thrown in the rubbish bin. Use washable cups and plates instead of paper or plastic cups and plates. Use cloth nappies for babies instead of disposable nappies.

To **reuse** means to use a resource for a purpose that is different to its original purpose. Reuse empty glass jars as vases or storage containers. Reuse old car tyres as garden borders. Reuse plastic bags from stores to hold rubbish. If you have disposable plastic cups, plates or utensils, don't throw them away after one use; wash them and reuse them. Repair things where possible instead of disposing of them and buying new ones. Hold a yard sale when you have things to get rid of; other people might find a use for items that you would otherwise throw away. Reuse gift paper for wrapping presents or covering books.

Increasingly in modern society, people are buying things from shops. The purpose of packaging is to contain, protect, identify and facilitate the sale and distribution of a consumer product. Virtually all manufactured and processed goods require packaging. The basic materials of packages today include paper, cardboard, cellophane, steel, aluminium, glass, wood, cloth and plastics. Excessive packaging is when too much or unnecessary material is used.

A shirt, for example, may be packaged in a cardboard box with a cellophane see-through front. Many pins are used to hold the shirt in place around a sheet of cardboard inside the shirt. Is all this packaging really necessary? Would you buy the same shirt if it were on a hanger in a shop?

Toys are often presented in colourful attractive boxes. A small baby's rattle or a model toy car, for example, may be packaged in a comparatively large box. The packaging is costly and adds nothing to the usefulness or quality of the product. If you had a choice, would you buy the same product in or out of a box? We should assume that the product would be cheaper if it was not in the box.

Packaging presents a major problem of environmental pollution. Millions of tonnes of packaging are discarded as rubbish each year. Some is biodegradable and some is not. Non-degradable material either does not decompose or decomposes very slowly in the natural environment.

In villages we may burn or bury our rubbish. In towns the council has a collection service to take rubbish to landfill areas. Here bulldozers compact the rubbish into layers and cover each layer with clean soil, which is also compacted. Another means of dealing with the problem is by recycling packaging materials for use as new products, packages and fuel.

Many of the papers and plastic material can be reused, recycled and reduced to minimise the pollution. Some recyclable items can be sold for cash. For example, empty drink cans can be crushed, bagged and sold as scrap metal. Other items can be used to beautify our school buildings. For example, old tyres can be used as simple borders around classroom buildings. Old newspapers can be sold to garages for spray painting purposes.

Leaves, cut grass and chicken manure can be mixed as compost and later applied to soil as fertiliser. Old paint tins can be reused as pots for ornamental plants and sold in markets for cash. Other waste products from locally produced or imported items can be reused. For example an old fuel drum or tank can be cut in half for growing vegetables. Broken furniture can be recycled and made into children's toys.

Environmentally friendly waste management practices benefit the environment. People have attractive, healthy environments to live in with clean air and water. There is a reduction in pollution, vermin and disease. Before dropping or throwing something on the ground, stop and think of a more appropriate action.

Environmental values

Environmentally friendly ways of managing the environment should reflect the economical, cultural and ecological values that people have for their natural, built and social resources.

People value the things they can obtain from their environments that they can use to gain a cash income. These include natural resources such as fruits and nuts that are gathered from the bush, vegetables grown in the garden, animals that are raised, fish from the sea, wood sold for firewood, timber to be carved into artefacts, fibres to be made into bilums and leaves that are woven into baskets.

People value the income they are able to obtain as business enterprises are established such as fishing projects, mining ventures, forestry projects, fish and meat canneries and industrial activities.

People value the things they can obtain from built environmental resources. These include services such as health, religion, education, transport, electricity and telephone; and goods such as tools, machines, vehicles, processed food, building supplies, books, outboard motors, cooking pots and fabric.

People value other people in their environment. They enjoy the companionship they get from family, relatives, friends and work colleagues. Law and order problems spoil the social environment and these are not valued.

People value the cultural practices that give them identity and self-esteem. The traditional taboos, ceremonies and sacred places are passed from one generation to the next so that people can appreciate and participate in society as true Melanesians.

People value the relationship between plants and animals and their physical and biological environment that sustains life on this planet. The ecosystems need to be protected if life on the planet is to survive for future generations.

Class projects

Choose projects from the list below that are appropriate for the school's local area and available resources. Set clear criteria for the satisfactory completion of tasks.

1. Plan and establish an eco-tourism project. Plan activities that tourists and visitors can do to appreciate the beauty of your environment (for example, bush walks, river rides, guided tours of local plants and land features). Consider fees you could charge and skills needed to be a tour guide.

2. Investigate and undertake practical ways to reduce, reuse and recycle waste from food consumption to benefit and improve the local environment.

3. Plant trees, fruit trees and timber trees around the school and the community.

4. Establish food gardens at the school and demonstrate soil conservation practices such as growing legumes, crop rotation, contouring, mulching.

5. Work closely with the community leaders to organise a special community clean-up by cutting long grass, removing weeds, trimming trees, sweeping around the church or other community building and picking up plastic bags and other waste products.

SUB-STRAND 3 Crop and animal management

Main ideas

The main ideas of this strand are for students to learn about the importance of farming crops and animals for their own consumption and for sale. Crops include vegetables and tree crops. Animals include both land and water animals. Students will develop understandings about the importance of improving food production and applying appropriate methods that are suitable to local conditions. Students plan, design and implement crop and animal projects to generate income and develop understandings of appropriate food processing and preservation practices.

The learning outcomes for each upper primary grade for this sub-strand are shown in the following table:

Grade 6	Grade 7	Grade 8
6.1.3 Students share an understanding of the economical, cultural and nutritional value of crops and animals and compare the benefits of traditional and commercial crop and animal management.	7.1.3 Students explain appropriate crop management and animal husbandry practices and demonstrate these through undertaking a practical project.	8.1.3 Students plan, design and implement a crop or animal project suited to local conditions and resources aimed at generating an income.

Key words

crops, animals, management, economical value, cultural value, nutritional value, traditional farming, commercial farming, appropriate practices, market needs, competitive strategies, targeted consumers, nursery, direct planting, weeding, mulching, irrigation, harvesting, processing, storage, biodiversity, soil type

Possible assessment tasks

Assessment aims to gather information on how well students achieve the learning outcomes for Sub-strand 3 (Crop and animal management). Clear criteria should be set for satisfactory completion of tasks.

The suggested activities are organised from simple school- or home-based activities (Grade 6 level) to more complex community-based ones (Grade 8 level); however, these levels are not prescriptive and teachers should choose activities according to students' needs and abilities.

Activities suitable for developing into assessment tasks include:

1. establish a herb garden with parsley, mint, chives, ginger, mustard, garlic, cardamom, chillies

2. grow a variety of crops such as yams, sweet potatoes, taro, cassava, pumpkin, corn, carrots, tomatoes, beans, peas, choko, aibika, lettuces, cabbages, broccoli, cauliflower, eggplants, peanuts, mushrooms, pitpit and capsicums

3 grow a variety of fruit such as bananas, pawpaws, pineapples, lemons, oranges, mangoes, guavas, avocado, custard apple, watermelons, passionfruit, cucumbers and laulaus

4 create a mini-zoo of local birds and animals

5 produce cash crops such as wheat, vanilla, cocoa, coffee, coconut, rubber, rice, oil palm, teak, pine and balsa

6 harvest and process sago

7 farm fish, crabs, prawns, lobsters, shell-fish, turtle; experiment with different ways of preparing them for sale

8 butterfly farming; bee keeping; raising rabbits, pigs, goats, sheep, cattle, horses, chickens; using modern slaughtering methods

9 give guided tours of farming enterprises.

Major links to other subjects

'Crop and animal management' builds upon learning in lower primary subjects such as Environmental Studies and Community Living. At the upper primary level, it links to the 'living things' strand of Science and the 'people and environment' strand of Social Science. These links are also noted as icons in the student books.

Teacher information

Types of crops and animals

Crops are all the plant produce from the land that is cultivated to meet human needs. It may be for personal use or to generate an income. Papua New Guinea has a great diversity of crops.

Crops include our staple foods such as sweet potatoes, yam, taro, cassava, sago, cooking bananas and white potatoes.

Common vegetables grown include pumpkin, corn, carrots, tomatoes, beans, peas, choko, aibika, capsicum, lettuces, cabbages, broccoli, cauliflower, eggplants, mushroom and *pitpit.*

Common fruits grown include eating bananas, pawpaws, pineapples, lemons, oranges, mangoes, guavas, avocado, custard apple, soursop, granadilla, pomelo, tree tomatoes, watermelons, passionfruit, cucumbers and laulaus. There is also a great variety of nuts.

Cash crops and forest trees that are grown primarily for export include vanilla, cocoa, coffee, coconut, rubber, rice, sugar cane, oil palm, teak, kwila, klinki pine, hoop pine and balsa.

Animals include all the living creatures of the air, sea and land that meet human needs in one way of another. Dogs and cats, for example, meet human needs for pets, companionship, protection or hunting. Pups and kittens from dogs and cats can be sold, particularly if they are popular breeds.

Birds also can be sold to generate an income. Some hotels have big cages for cassowaries, hornbills, cockatoos and *guria* pigeons. They are used as an attraction for guests to learn about fauna in Papua New Guinea. Some families may buy a bird as a family pet.

A wildlife sanctuary could be established at the school with a collection of local reptiles, birds and animals. As well as providing a learning opportunity for students, it could prove an attraction for visitors. However, the main focus of income-generating animal projects is related to animal husbandry. This is concerned with farming animals for food purposes.

From the waters of our rivers and seas we get all kinds of food. There are numerous varieties of fish such as tuna, trout, tilapia, carp, red emperor, barramundi, barracuda, eels and shark. Other water animals include octopus, dugong, turtle and crocodile. A variety of crustaceans include different shells, oysters, prawns, crabs and crayfish.

Land animals that are raised to provide food include chickens, pigs, goats, rabbits, sheep and cattle. Wildlife land animals that also provide food are cuscus, wallabies, bats, snakes and bandicoots.

Suggested activity

Conduct a survey to identify valuable crops and animals in the local area.

The value of crops and animals

Crops and animals are important in Papua New Guinea because of their economic, nutritional and cultural value.

Economic value

The economic value of crops and animals is that they may be used for personal purposes such as food, clothing and traditional dress, which provides a saving in what needs to be bought. They can also be sold to provide an income for individuals, families and the nation. Local markets are colourful and plentiful throughout the country and provide a valuable income for families. In the cash economy of modern society, people need income to buy goods they cannot produce and to pay for services such as health, education, travel, electricity and telephone. Local and export companies purchase cash crops from local growers. Cash crops such as coffee, cocoa, coconut, tea, rubber, timber, oil palm and vanilla are important for trade and export. Papua New Guinea exports its products to many countries throughout the world such as Australia, Japan, United Kingdom, America and Germany. Papua New Guinea has meat and fish canneries and sugar, tea and coffee factories.

Nutritional value

Crops and animals provide the food that enables us to have healthy bodies. Whether they are produced at home or bought from markets or shops, our diets are comprised of crop and animal foods. Humans have a great variety of food to choose from to meet their needs. We could not survive without the food that comes from crops and animals.

Consider the nutritional value of the crops and animals you plan to produce. The nutritional value of food is found in the food substances that the body can use for energy, warmth, the growth and repair of tissue, protection from diseases and the regulation of body processes. All of these functions occur when our bodies take in enough of the right kind of food to meet our needs. The substances in food are called 'nutrients' and the six nutrients are protein, carbohydrates, fats, vitamins, minerals and water.

Protein foods are all kinds of fish, seafood, animals, eggs, milk, peanuts and legumes (beans, peas). The body uses the protein in these foods to build and repair tissue. Protein foods are especially important for growing children and injured people. It should be noted that while these foods are rich sources of protein, they also contain other nutrients. Tinned fish, for example contains some fat, calcium, iron and vitamin B in addition to protein. Peanuts contain some carbohydrate, fat, fibre, calcium, iron and vitamin B in addition to protein.

There are three types of carbohydrate: sugar, starch and cellulose. Sugar is found in sugar cane and all sweet fruit. Starch is found in all our starchy staple foods such as potato, yam, taro, sago, rice, cassava, breadfruit and cooking bananas. Cellulose is the fibre in food. The body uses sugar and starch for energy and warmth. Even when we are asleep we need energy for our heart, lungs and other body systems to work and for our bodies to be warm at an even temperature. People who especially need energy foods are people who lead active lives such as young children, sports people and people who do physical labour. Fibre in foods is valuable to stimulate the digestive tract and enable our bowels to function properly.

Fats are found in oily and fatty food. The body uses fats for energy and warmth. Food sources of fats are coconut oil, cooking oils, margarine, butter, dripping, animal fat, some oily fish and avocado.

Important sources of vitamins and minerals are coloured fruits and vegetables. See the table on page 38 for more information.

Cultural value

Plants and animals are valued for aesthetic and cultural purposes. Plant and animal products are highly valued for personal adornment, traditional dress and ceremonial occasions. Dogs' teeth, animal bones, bird feathers, cuscus fur, turtle shell, kina shell and snake skin are just some of the animal products that form part of headdresses, pierced ears, pierced noses, neckbands, clothing and drum skins. Bark and numerous colourful leaves and flowers are plant sources for traditional dress that varies from culture to culture. Many provinces have 'shows' where a huge variety of different types of traditional dress are worn. Pigs have prestige and are important for feasts and ceremonies. Traditional crops and animals have always been important for trade, relationships between clans, bride price, compensation and celebrations.

The cultural value of food is at the heart of our everyday life. The food customs that are passed from one generation to the next highlight the uniqueness of the culture with which we identify. The cultural value of food is represented in the ways in which we:

- have a particular staple food like sago, yam, sweet potato or taro
- grow, hunt, fish or gather our food
- hold ceremonies to celebrate harvesting of crops or fish
- damage gardens in tribal fights in order to hurt others
- prepare food and the materials and equipment we use
- use food to acknowledge the status of a person or the importance of an event
- use food for births, deaths, compensation and bride price
- use food for curative or medicinal purposes

A variety of plant and animal substances are important in some cultures for traditional medical practices. Powders and potions may be drunk, inhaled or rubbed on the skin to treat rashes, sores, bruises, asthma, headaches, coughs, colds and other ailments. Many people in Papua New Guinea trust and try traditional medicines and treatments before resorting to Western methods.

Suggested activities

1. Conduct a survey to identify ways in which people obtain an income from crops and animals in the local area.
2. Consider the nutritional value of crops and animals and identify foods that are rich sources of different nutrients.
3. Interview community elders for information about the cultural value of food as passed on from one generation to the next through stories, celebrations and usage.
4. Plan a menu of daily meals using crops and animal sources produced in the local community.
5. Investigate crops and animals that are produced in another province or country.

6 Observe and ask questions to obtain information on income generated from sales of crops and animals in your locality.

7 Interview appropriate people in the community for information on traditional medicines, the plant and animal products that are used and the health problems they cure.

8 Examine the traditional dress of your locality. Identify the plant or animal materials used and how they are prepared. Plan a cultural day at which to wear traditional dress.

The benefits of traditional and introduced crops and animals

Of all the crops and animals in Papua New Guinea, some are traditional and some have been introduced. There are benefits or advantages for people from both traditional and modern crops and animals.

The benefits of traditional crops and animals are that they are suited to local conditions, resistant to diseases, sustained by familiar farming methods and used in ways to maintain cultural heritage. For generations people have developed effective ways of seed collection and propagation to sustain their food supply. Traditional crops and animals are also important for maintaining the local biodiversity. 'Bio' means life and 'diversity' means variety, so 'biodiversity' refers to the variety of plant and animal life forms living on Earth and the habitats or environments in which they live.

A benefit of modern crops and animals is that they provide a greater diversity of food for the meals that people eat. People have the advantage of greater choice and different flavours. Many of the modern crops and animals have commercial benefits for people, that is, they provide a monetary source of income. People have a greater variety of food to sell in markets and can attract a wider range of customers. Cash crops have export potential. Modern crops and animals are high yielding and have fast growth.

Many Papua New Guineans cultivate a mixture of traditional and modern crops and animals. Sometimes the best and greatest area of land is given to cash crops and poorer land is used for the family food crops. Sometimes the best food crops are taken to the market for sale and poorer food crops kept for family consumption. People need to make wise decisions in how their farming methods provide the greatest benefit to the family.

Suggested activities

1 Evaluate the benefits of traditional and commercial farming.

2 Make an informed decision about the farming system that would be most beneficial to families in your local area.

Traditional	Introduced
pigs seafood such as fish, crabs, crayfish, oysters, prawns, turtle, dugong sweet potato, yam, taro, sago, cassava bananas, breadfruit coconuts sugar cane wild fruit, berries, nuts	chickens cattle English potatoes, carrots, tomatoes, pumpkin, cucumber broccoli, cauliflower strawberries, pineapples, pawpaw coffee, tea, cocoa, oil palm, vanilla, rubber

Managing Resources

Appropriate crop management practices

Crop management practices include land preparation, planting methods such as nursery or direct planting, weeding, mulching, irrigation, harvesting, processing, storage, and pest and disease control.

Land preparation

Start with land choice and preparation. Choose a suitable site. Clear the land. Cut down weeds with bush knives and put them in a compost heap. Dig out big stumps, dead logs, shrubs and wild ferns. Turn over the soil with hoes and garden forks. Spread manure or compost evenly over the soil. Bury the manure or compost in the soil using hoes or spades. Green weeds can also be dug into the soil to add humus. Smooth the surface soil with a rake or spade. Consider how heavy rain may cause erosion and make drains where appropriate.

Planting methods

Two planting methods are to plant tiny seeds in trays in a nursery or to plant cuttings and larger seeds directly into the soil. Tiny seeds for cabbages, lettuces, carrots and tomatoes are suitable for planting in seed boxes. After they develop into seedlings, they can be transplanted into the prepared garden soil. Crops such as corn, pumpkin, beans, peas and peanuts have bigger seeds and these are suitable for planting directly into the prepared garden soil. Crops such as taro, yam, sweet potato, sugar cane, cassava, aibika and pitpit can be grown from cuttings that are planted directly into the soil.

Weeding

Regular weeding is needed to prevent plants competing with weeds for sunlight, water and soil nutrients. Also, many weeds carry organisms that infect crops and cause diseases. One method of removing weeds is simply hand-pulling them out of the ground or removing them by using a spade or hoe. A second effective method for weed control is mulching. Covering soil with mulch prevents weeds from germinating.

Mulching

Mulching is an appropriate crop management practice. As well as stopping weeds from growing, it prevents water from evaporating from the soil. It keeps the soil cool for seeds to grow. In addition to protecting the plants, mulch decays in time and enriches the soil. Digging in the decayed mulch enriches the qualities of the soil and makes a better environment for growing crops.

Irrigation

Plants need water to grow. Where the rainfall is insufficient, water needs to be supplied to the plants by people. This may be called *irrigation.* The most common method in Papua New Guinea is where people apply water from a bucket or hose. This is a time consuming and labour intensive method. However, irrigation systems can be installed that consist of pipes and sprinklers.

Harvesting

Harvesting is the time when crops are gathered in. Crops like tomatoes, pawpaws and bananas are harvested when the fruit is ripe. Crops like aibika, lettuces, cabbages and spinach are harvested when the leaves are mature and tender. Corn and beans are harvested when they mature. Root crops like carrots are harvested when the root is large enough but before it becomes woody and loses its sweetness. Potatoes, yam, cassava and taro are harvested when the tubers are large enough and are needed. Cash crops such as coffee, rubber, cocoa, coconut and vanilla are also harvested in particular ways.

Processing

After the food is harvested, it is processed in appropriate ways to be sold. Simple processing may involve only picking, sorting and washing fruits and vegetables before they are taken to market. Some processing methods convert raw materials into a different form or change the nature of the product. Crops such as sago, sugar cane, coffee, rubber, cocoa, coconut and vanilla have complex processes to prepare them for sale.

Storage

If crops are not used or sold quickly they need to be stored. All food crops should be stored in clean, dry places and checked regularly for damage. Damaged food should be removed to stop the damage from spreading to other food. Crops should be dry before they are stored; otherwise, mould and rot will quickly spoil the food. Insects, rats, mice and mould are enemies of stored produce.

Pest and disease control

Controlling pests and diseases is another aspect of appropriate crop and animal management. Plant your crops at the right time of the year when there are fewer insects. Digging your garden sometimes exposes larvae to the sun and they die. Rotate the crops so that the same plants are not always growing in the same place. Feed and water plants sufficiently so they will be more resistant to insects. When you first see the signs of diseased leaves, look for ways to get rid of them very quickly. As you walk around the garden, pick off and destroy any insects that you see. Problems are caused by insects, beetles, locusts, snails, weevils, rats, mice, fungi and bacteria. Insecticides and poisons can be used to control pests but these are poisonous and can affect humans.

Suggested activity

Apply appropriate crop management practices to a class food or cash crop project.

Appropriate animal husbandry practices

Animal husbandry is the agricultural practice of breeding and raising livestock. Appropriate practices include housing, feeding, choosing breeding stock, health of animals, hygiene, handling, slaughtering and processing.

Housing

Animal housing can be different shapes and sizes and made from different materials. The type of housing provided will depend on the livestock being kept, the resources available, locality and climate. Bush materials such as thatch roofs, bush timber walls and packed earthen floors may be used in some areas. Iron roofs, milled timber or chain wire walls and concrete floors may be used in other areas. Walls for pig houses need to be stronger than walls for chicken houses. Closed-in walls in the Highlands protect animals from cold, while coastal animal housing could be more open. A deep litter of straw or sawdust covers the floor for some animals. This collects animal waste and can be used later as compost for gardens. Special feeders and water containers can be purchased for chicken houses. A flow of air is necessary to minimise bad smells and help keep the area dry.

Feeding

To get the best results from your farm animals, they need to get enough feed and water. Water should be available at all times. If left to roam freely, animals can forage for the water and food they need. If you watch chickens, ducks, pigs or goats feeding around villages, you will see them eating leaves on plants, digging for worms, scratching for seeds and seeking other food sources. The animals you keep in captivity cannot find their own food. So the food they are given must provide a balanced diet. The amount of feed depends on the age and type of animal, the quality of the feed and the weather.

Choosing breeding stock

For healthy young animals with the characteristics we want, it is necessary to choose breeding stock with care. Our choice of breeding stock may be determined by availability of breeds, quantity, quality, cost, personal preference, climatic conditions, veterinary services, feeding requirements and other maintenance needs. Desired characteristics may include appearance, age, sex, egg-laying ability, quality of meat produced, rate of growth, resistance to diseases, absence of physical defects and fertility. By choosing to breed from stock with desirable characteristics, we promote the survival of those breeds and the possible extinction of other breeds.

Managing Resources

Protecting health

Appropriate animal husbandry practices are needed to protect the health of animals and prevent animal diseases. Provide good housing that is well protected from weather and has good ventilation. Make sure animal housing is clean and disinfected before bringing in new stock. Keep food and water supplies clean and clean containers regularly. Manage floor litter well to prevent the build-up of disease organisms. Provide enough good quality feed as malnourished animals have low resistance to diseases. Store feed in proper containers. Manage pest problems such as control methods for rats and mice. Always buy disease-free animals. Separate sick animals from healthy animals to prevent sickness spreading. Seek advice from a veterinarian (a doctor who treats animals) if health problems persist.

Handling

We need to take care in handling animals to prevent injuring the animal or ourselves. Wear appropriate protective clothing when handling animals. Keep the animal area clean and free of rubbish and sharp corners. Make your presence quietly known to avoid startling the animal. Avoid loud, abrupt noises that cause distress to livestock. Pens should be equipped with a gate. Livestock with young are usually more defensive and difficult to handle. When possible, let the young stay as close as possible to the adult when handling them. Livestock can be sold live, slaughtered or processed.

Slaughtering

All slaughtering should be done quickly to avoid undue suffering by the animal. Killing chickens or ducks can be done quickly by breaking the neck. Straight after killing, pluck, clean and rinse the bird. Pigs in Papua New Guinea are often killed by stunning. Animals are bled out after stunning to ensure that they die from loss of blood before there is a chance of them regaining consciousness.

Suggested activity

Apply appropriate animal husbandry practices to a class livestock project.

Class projects

Choose projects from the list below that are appropriate for the school's local area and available resources. Set clear criteria for the satisfactory completion of tasks.

1. Possible vegetable projects could be growing yams, sweet potatoes, taro, cassava, pumpkin, corn, carrots, tomatoes, beans, peas, choko, aibika, lettuces, cabbages, broccoli, cauliflower, eggplants, peanuts, mushrooms and pitpit.
2. Possible fruit projects could be growing bananas, pawpaws, pineapples, lemons, oranges, mangoes, guavas, avocado, custard apple, watermelons, passionfruit, cucumbers and laulaus.
3. Possible cash crop projects could be growing vanilla, cocoa, coffee, coconut, rubber, rice, teak, pine and balsa.
4. Possible animal projects could be farming fish or raising chickens, pigs, goats, rabbits, sheep and cattle.
5. In a sago area, students could harvest and process sago.

Use the Making a Living process of 'investigate, plan or design, make or produce, market or use, evaluate' as the framework for any class project.

Investigate—Plan to implement a crop or animal project. Look at crops and animals being sold by local people. Discuss strengths, weaknesses, opportunities and threats (a SWOT analysis) of food, livestock and cash crop projects. Explore economic opportunities. Use imagination and brainstorm ideas for crop or animal projects that complement those already in existence or provide something new. Gather information on the needs or wants of the community. Identify available resources and sources of expertise. Consider possible sites and inspect them. Consider options and identify suitable crop or animal projects for local conditions.

Plan or design—Develop an action plan. Clearly describe the project and its purpose. Explain the production process and the desired product to be sold. Estimate a time frame. Plan activities in a logical sequence. Choose appropriate equipment and resources needed to undertake a project. Calculate costs and estimated income. Design records to be kept. Identify activities to control and monitor quality. Consider the availability of labour and time.

Make or produce—Make garden beds or animal housing. Obtain seeds, plant cuttings or suitable breeding stock. Apply appropriate crop or animal management practices. Use equipment correctly and safely. Manage time and resources efficiently. Monitor and control quality. Adapt ideas and plans in response to constraints and difficulties. Apply post-harvest processing techniques. Maintain a regular supply of your product to meet market needs.

Market or use—Develop and use competitive marketing strategies. Package products hygienically and attractively. Calculate selling process. Use a range of selling techniques. Advertise and sell products to targeted consumers. Keep records of expenses and sales. Determine profit or loss.

Evaluate—Determine whether the project had a successful outcome. Reflect on the choice of the project, the processes involved and the products. Identify successes, failures and constraints. Analyse the viability of the project. Consider whether to continue, make improvements or try something new.

STRAND 2

Better Living

Better Living

About this strand

Learning in the Better Living strand is concerned with student development of skills and knowledge for the effective management of time, money, work, effort and resources to achieve a healthy, safe and productive lifestyle. The strand focuses on hygiene and nutrition for good health; care and management for a healthy and safe home and environment; money management to be a wise consumer; and creative and innovative ways to make things. Students develop problem-solving and decision-making skills and apply these in practical and real-life situations for better living.

The four sub-strands of the Better Living strand are:

- healthy living
- care and management
- wise consumer
- making things

There is one learning outcome for each sub-strand for each grade. The learning outcomes are broad and can be achieved in any context depending on available resources and expertise. Elaborating on the learning outcomes generates ideas that help the teacher to identify content and activities, possible projects and assessment tasks. From the learning outcome elaborations, teachers can write units of work and teaching programs relevant to the community served by the school.

The following is a sample elaboration of the Grade 6 learning outcome. The ideas are not exhaustive and teachers are encouraged to develop their own.

Example of elaborating a learning outcome

Grade: 6

Strand: Better Living

Sub-strand: Healthy living

Learning outcome: *6.2.1 Describe and demonstrate aspects of personal hygiene, nutrition and safety that promote a healthy lifestyle.*

Four key areas can be derived from this outcome: healthy lifestyle, personal hygiene, aspects of good nutrition and safety. Each area can be elaborated.

For example, the area of aspects of good nutrition can be elaborated as follows:

- Describe the functions of nutrients in the body. Role play being nutrients in food: protein (vegetable and animal); carbohydrates (sugar, starch and cellulose); fats (from plants and animals); vitamins (A, B, C, D, E); minerals (iron, calcium); water. Investigate availability of local food sources of nutrients (excursions to gardens, shops and markets).

- Investigate health problems caused when a nutrient in lacking. Listen to a health worker talk about causes and cases of malnutrition (kwashiorkor, marasmus, obesity, being underweight). Observe, identify and assess signs of good and poor nutrition.
- Describe balanced meals. Identify combinations of various protein, staple and coloured vegetable meals. Plan a variety of balanced meals for breakfast, lunch and dinner. Collect data and evaluate student lunches. Maintain a journal of food eaten in a week. Conduct interviews with town and village residents on food preferences for balanced meals. Plan vegetarian meals that are nutritionally balanced. Estimate costs of various balanced meals for families. Collect recipes.
- Collect information on traditional and modern methods of cooking: smoking, grilling, mumu, aigir, boiling, stewing, drying, baking, roasting, steaming. Observe and use different types of cooking places: open fires, hot stones, ground ovens, barbecue plates, drum ovens, kerosene primuses, wood stoves, electric stoves, gas stoves. Handle utensils appropriately and safely. Prepare food using different cooking methods. Compare moist and dry heat methods. Consider nutritional snacks and lunches that could be sold at school.

From the ideas generated, the teacher can decide on appropriate topics to include in a unit of work, taking into account students' prior knowledge, food resources in the locality and expertise available. The elaboration provides ideas of topics to investigate and activities for students to do.

The *time allocation* for Making a Living is 360 minutes per week. This allows time for practical activities and students to get out of the classroom to investigate and gather information. An example is shown in the following table:

Monday	Tuesday	Wednesday	Thursday	Friday
2pm–3pm Survey food likes and dislikes of children.	1pm–3pm Walk around, observe and ask questions on available food, utensils and cooking places.	2pm–3pm Plan nutritious drinks, snacks and lunches.	8am–10am Prepare nutritious drinks, snacks and lunches to sell at affordable prices.	

Assessment is an ongoing process and should be carried out as students undertake activities. Possible assessment ideas for the above example may include:

- role play being a particular nutrient demonstrating why you are needed and what happens if you are not eaten in sufficient quantity
- list observations of foods available in local gardens, markets and stores according to their main nutritional value
- write recipes using a variety of garden, market and store foods
- plan nutritious drinks, snacks and lunches for children and design suitable hygienic packaging
- demonstrate food preparation skills such as peeling, washing, cutting, chopping, grating, boiling, grilling
- demonstrate safe and appropriate use of cooking equipment
- plan and implement a project to prepare and sell nutritious food
- evaluate the benefit of the project for healthy living

SUB-STRAND 1 # Healthy living

Main ideas

The main ideas of the 'healthy living' sub-strand are for students to develop knowledge and skills for maintaining and promoting a healthy way of living and for identifying factors contributing to unhealthy lifestyles. Students demonstrate skills for being clean themselves, and having clean clothes, buildings and grounds. They demonstrate awareness of safety practices. They apply traditional and introduced methods of food preparation, processing and preservation and plan and prepare nutritious meals for personal consumption or for sale.

The learning outcomes for 'healthy living' are shown in the following table:

Grade 6	Grade 7	Grade 8
6.2.1 Describe and demonstrate aspects of personal hygiene, nutrition and safety that promote a healthy lifestyle.	7.2.1 Analyse aspects of a nutritious diet and suggest how and where they might obtain, preserve, process and prepare these foods to meet nutritional requirements.	8.2.1 Investigate and implement practical ways to produce and prepare food for personal consumption or to generate an income.

Key words

nutrients, food groups, balanced meals, malnutrition, hygiene, safety, lifestyle, diet, preserve, processing, utensils, cooking methods, handling, packaging, cater, laundry, consumption

Possible assessment tasks

Assessment aims to gather information on how well students achieve the learning outcomes for Sub-strand 1 (Healthy living). Clear criteria should be set for satisfactory completion of tasks.

The suggested activities are organised from simple school- or home-based activities (Grade 6 level) to more complex community-based ones (Grade 8 level); however, these levels are not prescriptive and teachers should choose activities according to students' needs and abilities.

Activities suitable for developing into assessment tasks include:

1 publish a recipe book for nutritious snacks and balanced meals

2 use different cooking methods to prepare food

3 arrange food and set tables for different occasions

4 make toothbrush holders, bamboo combs, toiletry bags, first-aid kits for travelling

5 build a tool rack, hanging hooks, cupboard or other storage facility

Better Living

6 provide a laundry service, demonstrating skills of sorting, soaking, washing, rinsing, wringing, drying, ironing and folding

7 provide a cleaning service for home, buildings or grounds, demonstrating skills of tidying, dusting, sweeping, mopping, wiping, neat storage and waste disposal

8 provide a clothes repair service, demonstrating skills of replacing buttons, patching, darning and mending seams

9 plan a variety of catering menus and cater for a function, serving or packaging food cleanly and attractively

10 offer hairdressing services such as styling, cutting and dyeing

11 sell nutritious food, such as fruity ice cups, stick food, boiled eggs, fresh fruit, stuffed bananas, sandwiches, slices of fresh fruit, doughnuts, cakes, sausage bites

Major links to other subjects

'Healthy living' builds upon student learning in lower primary subjects, in particular Health and Community Living. At the upper primary level, 'healthy living' has major links to the 'science in the home' and 'living things' sub-strands in Science and the 'movement and physical activity' and 'health of individuals and population' sub-strands in Personal Development. These links are noted as icons in the student books.

Better Living

Teacher information

Process skills

The Make a Living process applied to the 'healthy living' sub-strand has these components:

Investigation—Through observing, asking questions and making comparisons, students investigate differences between healthy and unhealthy lifestyles and factors that contribute to these situations.

Planning and designing—Students plan and design products and services that promote healthy lifestyles. Through having a clear purpose and considering costs, resources, options and possible constraints, action plans such as mending clothes or selling food are developed. Plans can relate to clean environment, personal cleanliness, exercise, hygiene, nutrition or safety.

Making or producing—Working individually or collaboratively, plans for healthy living activities are translated into practice. As students develop their products, they develop skills of effective time, resource and quality management.

Marketing or using—Marketing requires students to apply marketing strategies to sell their healthy living products. Some healthy living services, such as picking up rubbish or watching over children on school crossings, are not saleable and can be implemented as free community services.

Evaluating—Evaluation requires students to make judgments about the processes and outcomes of their planned healthy living activities. They identify strengths, weaknesses and constraints and suggest improvements for further activities.

Healthy lifestyle

A healthy lifestyle provides opportunity for people to interact positively with each other, and to develop physically, mentally and socially to their fullest potential in order to live productively. An unhealthy lifestyle prevents a person from achieving their optimum development and lessens their ability to be productive citizens.

Healthy people

Signs of a healthy person include high levels of energy, a good appetite, firm muscles, clear skin, weight in proportion to height and age, alert eyes and springy hair. A healthy person can participate in everyday activities without getting tired and finds time to relax and enjoy leisure activities. An unhealthy person gets infections or sicknesses easily, has dull eyes, thin muscles and low levels of energy, is overweight or underweight and gets tired doing everyday activities.

Healthy environment

A healthy environment is one that is clean, pest-free, not littered, attractive, free of violence, well lit and airy, and has enough space for the number of people occupying it. Unhealthy environments may be polluted with plastic bags, betel nut spit, graffiti, vehicle fumes, animal droppings, rusty tins, broken bottles and building debris.

Healthy lifestyle

Our lifestyles are reflected in different ways of living, dressing, maintaining hygiene, types of food, trade, spiritual beliefs, building styles, leisure activities, ways of earning income, and access to shops, electricity, roads, water, health and education services. Over time, changes occur in our physical, social and economic environments, and this can have positive and negative effects on people and the community.

One example of change is that traditional costumes have given way to modern fabric clothes for everyday wear. On the one hand, modern clothes can be washed, are available in a range of colours and styles, last for years if cared for and are suitable for travel to different provinces and overseas. On the other hand, modern clothes can be expensive and cash is needed. For a healthy lifestyle, people should dress appropriately for different occasions. If it is a cultural day, traditional clothing is worn with great pride in our unique cultural heritage. If it is a normal school day, we wear comfortable, appropriate, modern clothing.

Suggested activity

Students can conduct a survey to gather information on lifestyle changes that have occurred in the community. They can then write a report on positive and negative effects of changes on community lifestyles.

Personal hygiene

Personal hygiene is an essential part of healthy living. Skin should be washed to make people feel clean and fresh, prevent bad body smells and remove dust, dirt, grease, dry skin and stale sweat. Each person should wash all over at least once a day, paying special attention to the armpits and body creases. Hands are washed more often, also paying attention to having clean fingernails. Diarrhoea is common and is caused by germs being passed from the hands to the food that enters the body. Scabies is a skin problem that occurs when the skin is not washed often enough. Water and soap are used to keep the skin clean. A clean bath towel is used for drying the body.

Head lice are a common problem in people's hair. If untreated, the lice burrow in the skin and cause itchiness and infected sores on the scalp. Lice-killing substances can be purchased. A common method is to apply the solution and leave it on the hair for twenty-four hours before washing it out. This kills all the live lice but does not kill the louse eggs that are glued to strands of hair. One week later, the procedure needs to be repeated to kill newly hatched lice. By regularly washing our hair with shampoo and using clean combs, we can usually avoid getting head lice.

Teeth are kept clean by brushing with toothpaste on a toothbrush, at least once a day.

Teeth are cleaned to remove soft food like sweet potato, rice and cake that stick to surfaces of the teeth. Unclean teeth look unattractive and decay more easily. Eating firm vegetables and fruits such as carrot, cucumber, watermelon, laulau and coconut helps to remove clinging food and keep teeth clean.

Sneezes, coughs and colds are common, particularly in the colder highland areas of Papua New Guinea. It is polite to cover your mouth when you sneeze or cough to prevent your germs and breath going onto other people. It is unsightly to see mucus from the nose sitting on the upper lips of people or being licked into the mouth. Also, it is unhygienic to see nasal mucus being squirted on the ground. The correct procedure is to cover the nose with a paper tissue or handkerchief and blow the mucus out of the nostrils. If using paper tissues, ensure you dispose of them thoughtfully.

When clothes are new, we feel proud of them. The colours are bright and the clothes feel nice to wear. After they are worn a few times, they absorb sweat, get dirty and smelly and lose their freshness. If clothes are washed and cared for, they can look like new again and you can be proud of them. While outer clothes may be worn more than once before washing, underclothes should only be worn once and then washed.

'Laundering' is the term using for the processes used in washing clothes. The hand-washing processes are as follows. First collect the clothes to be washed. Check to see if any of the clothes need mending. It is better to mend broken clothes before washing as the handling may make the damage worse. Soak clothes to loosen the dirt so that the washing will take less time, require less rubbing and use less soap. Do not soak coloured clothes if you think the colour will run. White clothing can be soaked in a bleach solution. After some time, get clean water and wash each item of clothing by rubbing soap over the fabric surface. Wring the clothing with a twisting action. Rinse the soapy water from the clothing and wring again to remove excess water. Clothes may be spread on the ground to dry or hung on lines. Animals and children may walk on clothes on the ground, so it may be better to put them on lines. The use of clothes pegs helps keep the clothes from falling or being blown off lines. When the clothes are dry, remove them from the lines and fold them neatly. Most people in this country do not have irons. However, if you have an electric iron, you can iron the clothes and place them on hangers. Store clothes in a clean, pest-free place.

Good nutrition

Nutrition refers to the processes by which the food taken into the body is converted to living tissue, and used for warmth, energy and the protection and regulation of body functions. Scientists have studied food and learned about its nutritional content. Sometimes we classify nutrients into six groups: protein, carbohydrates, fats, vitamins, minerals and water. Sometimes we classify the nutrients into three groups according to their functions in the body: growth, energy and protection.

Growth

The body uses protein for growth and repair of tissues. There are animal and plant sources of protein. Animal sources include fresh and tinned meat, fresh and tinned fish, all seafood, pork, chicken, lamb, milk, eggs, birds, wallabies and ducks. Plant sources of protein include wing beans, soya beans, snake beans, peas, peanuts, pandanus and nuts. People who only get their protein from plant sources are called 'vegetarians'.

Energy

The body uses fats and carbohydrates for energy and warmth. For equal quantities of food, fats have twice the energy value of carbohydrates; however, we usually only eat fats in very small quantities. Fats are found in all greasy food, oils, margarine and dripping. On the other hand, we eat carbohydrate food in much larger quantities. The three types of carbohydrates are sugars, starches and cellulose. Sugars are found in sweet foods like sugar cane and sweet fruits. Starches are found in all our root vegetables (potato, yam, taro, cassava), rice, sago, bananas, breadfruit, flour products and corn. The main starchy food eaten by someone is their 'staple' food. Cellulose is the fibre in food. While cellulose has little nutritional value, it is important to provide the bulk of waste that passes out of the body as faeces.

Protection

The body uses vitamins and minerals for protection against infection and regulation of body functions:

Vitamin/mineral	Sources	Information
Vitamin A	carrots, pumpkin, sweet potatoes, broccoli, dark green leafy vegetables	• helps form and maintain healthy teeth, skeletal and soft tissue, mucous membranes and skin • promotes good vision
Vitamin B group	cereals, fish, meat, beans, peas, fruits, nuts, milk, vegetables	• helps release the energy from energy foods
Vitamin C	citrus fruits (oranges and lemons), strawberries, tomatoes, broccoli, greens, and sweet and white potatoes	• builds up the body's resistance to infection • good for healthy gums, teeth, bones and healing of wounds
Vitamin D	oily fish, eggs, milk, cereals	• good for strong bones and teeth • made by the body on exposure to light
Vitamin E	corn, nuts, seeds, green leafy vegetables	• important for the formation of red blood cells and the use of vitamin K. It is found in corn, nuts, seeds and green leafy vegetables.
Vitamin K	cabbage, cauliflower, spinach, soya beans and cereals	• helps blood to clot when bleeding occurs
Iron	meat, fish, nuts and green leafy vegetables	• makes blood and prevents the blood disease anaemia
Calcium and phosphorus	milk and dairy products, broccoli, legumes	• help build strong bones and teeth
Iodine	iodised salt, seafood	• prevents goitre and is needed for the thyroid gland hormone

'Diet' is a term that refers to the usual or regular food people choose to eat. A balanced diet or a balanced meal is one that contains all the nutrients. For the sake of simplicity, we say a balanced meal has some food from each of the three food groups. Here are some examples: meat, sweet potato and coloured vegetables; fish, rice and coloured vegetables; or a stew of chicken, noodles and coloured vegetables. Eating fruit and nuts provides nutritious snacks between meals.

For good health it is important that meals are nutritious and prepared in hygienic ways. Using a variety of cooking methods and food makes meals more interesting and enjoyable for people to eat.

Cooking methods may be classified as moist and dry methods. Moist cooking methods use water and include boiling, stewing, mumu and steaming. Dry cooking methods use no water and include frying, grilling, smoking, baking and roasting.

Suggested activities

Practical activities for learning about good nutrition are essential. Where resources are scarce, teachers need to be innovative. If you can grow flowers at your school, you can grow food plants. Consider planting corn, aibika, tomatoes, peanuts or other food for practical activities in gardens instead of flowers. If land is a problem, use empty drums or old tanks as containers for growing food producing plants. As a low cost activity, you could use a root vegetable like sweet potato to cook in different ways (for example, boiled, fried, mashed, sliced in different ways and fried, roasted, stuffed, coated in batter, mashed and coated in breadcrumbs and fried, or as potato cakes, potato wedges or chips).

Safety

The important thing about being safe or free from harm is awareness. People need to be aware of the potential for harm occurring before it occurs. If people are aware of the possibility of harm, they can take appropriate action and behave carefully and responsibly.

There are many situations where nothing bad has happened but where there is a chance that something bad could happen. Examples of hazardous situations include: not wearing a seat belt, standing in the back of a moving vehicle, projecting handles of saucepans, throwing sticks or stones, climbing trees, walking alone, being in a building when the door is unlocked, throwing a bottle on the ground that then smashes, sailing in a dinghy in rough seas, being near a drunk person, diving into shallow water, walking across flooded creeks, sitting under a coconut tree, using harmful substances without following the directions on the label, being near fire, walking with your back to oncoming traffic, handling sharp equipment, children putting small objects in their mouths, eating fish with bones, putting plastic bags over someone's head, teasing people in a way that could lead to fights, having unsafe sex and working with electrical fittings. For each one of these, there is an appropriate form of behaviour to prevent an accident happening.

Before teaching about safety, collect information on dangerous situations in your locality or province. Research these in order to plan children's learning in a meaningful way.

Lack of clean water can cause diarrhoea. Water polluted with human faeces can cause typhoid. Walking on ground where people have defecated can cause hookworm infections. Rubbish scattered on the ground attracts vermin that spread diseases and affect people's health. Inadequate ventilation in buildings can lead to breathing problems and the spread of sicknesses like coughs and colds. Poisonous animals and plants cause sickness or death. Some insects and plants cause stings that can become infected. All these and more can be harmful to a person's health and well-being.

Make links between causes and effects of behaviour. Describe effects of certain behaviours. Assess the risks of harm in different situations. Identify appropriate forms of behaviour to be safe. Compare causes and effects of behaviour.

Class projects

1 Implement a clothes repair or laundry service. Develop skills of replacing buttons, patching, darning and mending seams. Plan procedures for recording receipt of clothes and doing the washing or mending tasks. Advertise services at affordable fees. Maintain records. Get feedback from customers on the quality of services provided and areas for improvement.

2 Investigate client needs for a home, building or grounds cleaning service. Develop skills of waste disposal, tidying, dusting, sweeping, washing, mopping, wiping and neat storage. If not commercially viable, plan the project as a voluntary service to the community.

3 Plan and prepare a variety of nutritious food items, package in hygienic ways and sell to schoolchildren. These could be items such as fruity ice cups, stick food, sausage and tomato sandwiches, boiled eggs, fresh fruit or stuffed bananas. Estimate costs, determine selling prices and present for sale at suitable times in appropriate locations. Maintain records.

4 Investigate needs for improved neat and safe storage of tools, equipment, chemicals and cleaning agents. Respond as appropriate by building a tool rack, hanging hooks or other storage facility and labelling of the storage areas.

5 Identify special occasions for which the class could cater. It could involve making finger food such as sandwiches, slices of fresh fruit, doughnuts, cakes or sausage bites for a morning tea when visitors come to the school. It could include table decorations, making flower leis and providing tea, coffee or cold drinks. Let the head teacher or community leaders know that your class can provide the service, and set fees per person according to the menu or service provided.

SUB-STRAND 2 Care and management

Main ideas

The main ideas of the 'care and management' sub-strand are for students to investigate areas within the school and community that need improvement and to carry out appropriate activities to create a well-maintained, clean, attractive and safe place in which to learn, play and live. Students undertake activities to repair tables, chairs, shelves and desks, to maintain cleanliness of their surroundings and improve physical aspects of their environment.

The learning outcomes for 'care and management' are shown in the following table:

Grade 6	Grade 7	Grade 8
6.2.2 Develop an awareness of the importance of effective management skills in creating pleasant and safe environments at home and school and apply and make suggestions for improvement.	7.2.2 Assess home and school buildings to identify areas that require maintenance, repair and other improvements and undertake appropriate actions.	8.2.2 Work collaboratively with others to select and undertake a project based on identified needs within the school or community.

Key words

care, management, repair, interior decorations, beautification, furniture, efficiency, productivity, landscaping, resources, facilities, tools, equipment, techniques, plumbing, carpentry, building maintenance, improvisation

Possible assessment tasks

Assessment aims to gather information on how well students achieve the learning outcomes for Sub-strand 2 (Care and management). Clear criteria should be set for satisfactory completion of tasks.

The suggested activities are organised from simple school- or home-based activities (Grade 6 level) to more complex community-based ones (Grade 8 level); however, these levels are not prescriptive and teachers should choose activities according to students' needs and abilities.

Activities suitable for developing into assessment tasks include:

1. make cleaning items such as brushes and brooms from bush materials
2. sweep; clean walls, floor and louvres
3. decorate the interior of a room; make curtains, chair covers, pictures and picture frames, vases and wall hangings; rearrange furniture
4. paint a wall mural or interior and exterior walls of buildings
5. fix goalposts on sports fields
6. maintain a clean, tidy and well-organised tool shed; repair rakes and wheelbarrows; sharpen bush knives
7. landscape around buildings, cut grass, trim trees, make and weed food and flower gardens, plant trees, build seats, construct drains
8. sand and revarnish desks; repair steps, railings, desks or seats, broken furniture; repaint walls; replace door hinges
9. construct paths, foot bridges, bamboo bridges over streams
10. offer a cleaning service to sweep inside and outside; clean floor, louvres, toilets, kitchen; wash up dirty utensils; arrange furniture neatly; dispose of rubbish in appropriate places; keep desks clean and tidy.

Major links to other subjects

'Care and management' builds upon student learning in lower primary subjects, in particular Health and Community Living. At the upper primary level, care and management has major links to the 'community health' sub-strand in Personal Development and the 'environment and resources' sub-strand in Social Science. These links are noted as icons in the student books.

Teacher information

Diversity in what we need to care for

Care and management of what we have prolongs its usefulness and attractiveness. This includes anything and everything in our homes, schools, community buildings and their surrounding environment. Not only should we be concerned to maintain what we have, but also to consider ways to improve what we have.

There is great diversity in Papua New Guinea and teachers need to plan children's learning to be relevant to the buildings and environment of their locality. Specific methods and techniques for maintaining buildings will vary according to the construction materials used.

Buildings may be built of bush materials, with woven walls and thatched roofs. They may be on stilts with steps, over water or on the ground. They often have water from wells or streams, lighting by kerosene lamps, pit toilets, push-out leaf windows, open fires for cooking, bed mats on the floor and benches for storage.

Buildings may be built of permanent materials. These could be milled timber, bricks, concrete blocks, fibro, iron, steel and glass. Modern buildings often have a water and electricity supply, flushing toilets, glass windows, security wire, insect screen wire, polished floors, painted walls, stoves, refrigerators, washing machines, rotary clothes lines, beds, tables, chairs, sinks, mirrors, showers, iron roofs, cupboards and fences.

The diversity of locations also affects the types of buildings and environments we have. Locations include rural and urban, village and town, Highlands, islands, coastal and inland.

Resources for maintaining what we have will vary. In towns, people may readily access brooms, mops, dustpans, rubbish bins, brushes, insect sprays, rat traps, vacuum cleaners, polish, paint, many types of cleaning aids, sponge cloths, disinfectant, detergent, bar soap, soap powders, steel wool, nails, screws, tie-wire, hammers, chainsaws, electrical equipment and buckets.

In rural areas, people tend to have less access to modern aids for care and maintenance of buildings. Much ingenuity is applied to improvise ways and methods to carry out maintenance, repair and improvements.

Pleasant and safe home and school environments

Wherever we live and whatever facilities are there, everyone probably likes to live in a pleasant and safe environment. Students can identify pleasant and unpleasant, safe and unsafe environments by visiting different locations around the school and in the nearby community. They can express their views on criteria for a pleasant and safe environment. The following is one example, but this could vary according to personal preferences and location.

A pleasant environment in which to live and learn is clean, accident free, comfortable, attractive, inviting, free from pests and large enough for the number of people who occupy it. It provides shelter from rain, heat and cold. It provides protection from dangerous insects, animals, enemies and *raskols*. It has somewhere private for body washing and toilet purposes. It has a good supply of clean water and electricity for lighting and electrical equipment. It has somewhere to store, prepare, cook and eat food with labour saving equipment and appropriate furnishings. There are clean, well-constructed areas for storing belongings. It is well ventilated with screened windows to keep out mosquitoes that can cause malaria. Doors can be locked. It has a neat and tidy arrangement of furniture. It has a pleasant area where family and friends can relax, sit, talk, listen to music or watch television.

Outside the buildings there is a pleasant view. There are shady trees, neat flower and food gardens, cut lawns and paths. At school there are well-maintained playing fields with suitable markings and goal posts. For additional safety there may be security wire on windows, a security fence around the premises and security officers who patrol.

Areas requiring maintenance and repair

- Identify buildings in your locality. These could include houses, churches, community hall, classrooms, staff room and toilet blocks.
- Identify parts of a building that could require maintenance or improvement. These could include roof, gutters, water pipes, walls, verandah, steps, railings, doors, ceiling, floors, windows, louvres, tank and taps.
- Identify rooms in a house and fittings that could require maintenance or improvement. These could include bathroom (shower, handbasin, taps, mirror, toilet), bedroom (beds, cupboards), kitchen (table, chairs, sink, taps, benches, cupboards, rubbish bin), living room (tables, chairs, bookshelves, wall decorations).
- Identify outside areas that could require maintenance or improvement. These could include playing fields, goal posts, trees,

gardens, fences, grass, paths, storage sheds, haus win, waste disposal areas, cooking areas and clothes lines.

Assess needs

Some repair jobs require a qualified electrician, plumber or carpenter. Some jobs are costly and beyond the limit of your resources. In assessing areas that need maintenance and repair, keep in mind the limit of skills and resources.

Long grass needs cutting. Leaves on the grass need raking. Overgrown gardens need weeding. Overhanging branches of trees need trimming. Rubbish on the ground needs picking up. Burnable rubbish needs burning. Organic rubbish needs to be placed in compost heaps. Graffiti, dirt and mould on walls need to be removed by scrubbing. Holes in tanks or walls need patching. Dusty furniture or windows need dusting and wiping over with a damp cloth. Spider webs and wasp nests need removing. Dirty floors need sweeping and mopping. Untidy desks or storage areas need to be made neat and tidy. Leaking taps need to have their washers replaced. Swampy areas may need drains to be dug or to be filled in with stones or soil. Missing louvres need to be replaced with new ones. Broken fences need to be mended. Loose floorboards, steps or railings may need replacing or nailing to make firm again.

In addition to maintaining existing structures, consideration should be given to how they can be improved and beautified. Old or dangerous trees could be chopped down. New trees can be planted in chosen positions. New flower and food gardens can be made. Paths and footbridges can be upgraded by giving them a better surface. Seating could be built under shady areas. New tablecloths, curtains or chair covers could be sewn. Some desks and furniture may need to be sanded and revarnished. Some ceilings and walls may need re-painting. An extension to a building could be constructed. Furniture in a room could be rearranged. A new and better system for waste disposal could be created. Establish a nursery. Make vases and place fresh flowers in them.

Activities for everyday maintenance

Pick up rubbish. Dispose of rubbish thoughtfully. Reuse, recycle and reduce waste wherever possible. Sweep inside and outside. Tidy desks. Rake leaves. Cut grass. Weed gardens. Clean walls, windows and floors. Make beds. Wash used utensils. Place things where they belong. Arrange furniture neatly. Manage time efficiently by planning jobs and using appropriate techniques. Prevent accidents by moving potentially hazardous things out of harm's way. Use cleaning materials in an economic manner. Store materials and equipment safely and neatly in appropriate places. Save money by doing jobs regularly and fixing things when damage is small. All these caring and maintenance tasks help to keep our environment pleasant and safe.

Better Living

Class projects

Choose projects from the list below that are appropriate for the school's local area and available resources. Set clear criteria for the satisfactory completion of tasks.

1 Plan a classroom or school improvement program. It could involve painting a wall mural, decorating the interior of a room, rearranging furniture, making vases by reusing or recycling something, maintaining flower beds, landscaping around the school, disposing of rubbish in appropriate places, fixing goal posts on sports fields or digging drains. Implement and evaluate your work.

2 Assess the waste disposal standards at the school and in the surrounding

environment. Plan a project to improve waste disposal practices. It could be preparing and painting rubbish drums, building stands for rubbish drums, collecting litter from grounds and waterways or making signs to keep the environment beautiful.

3 Investigate the standard of water supply at the school, in homes nearby or in the community. Identify areas for improvement and possible projects to undertake. It could be repairing gutters and damaged water pipes, replacing washers on leaking taps or building soak pits or drains.

4 Identify care and maintenance needs of school or community buildings. Develop a plan of action to meet needs. Consider resources such as time, cost, money, materials, tools and facilities. Tasks could involve sweeping; cleaning walls, floor and louvres; repairing steps, railings, desks or seats; sanding and revarnishing desks; repainting walls; replacing door hinges. Use improvised ways and methods to carry out maintenance, repair and improvements. Make brushes and brooms from bush materials. Implement and evaluate the work.

SUB-STRAND 3 Wise consumer

Main ideas

The main ideas of the 'wise consumer' sub-strand are for students to develop skills of effective money management and to be able to make informed decisions about the goods and services that are available for them to access. Students demonstrate skills of effective money management, budget planning and record-keeping. They demonstrate awareness of consumer rights and responsibilities. They explore organisations that provide goods and services used by their families. They develop an understanding of the marketing, communication and management skills needed to satisfy consumer needs and to run a successful business.

The learning outcomes for 'wise consumer' are shown in the following table:

Grade 6	Grade 7	Grade 8
6.2.3 Describe the importance of effective money management, record-keeping and budget planning and apply this to a practical situation at home and school.	7.2.3 Investigate consumer rights and responsibilities and demonstrate practical ways to be a wise consumer.	8.2.3 Evaluate those goods and services that are provided by a range of organisations and make informed decisions about those that best meet their needs.

Key words

wisdom, money, mismanagement, budget, economy, consumer, rights, responsibilities, business records, business organisations, profit, income, expenses, cash flow, marketing, advertising, public relations, goods, products, services, needs, wants, rental, savings, sales, accountability, debt, loans

Possible assessment tasks

Assessment aims to gather information on how well students achieve the learning outcomes for Sub-strand 3 (Care and management). Clear criteria should be set for satisfactory completion of tasks.

The suggested activities are organised from simple school- or home-based activities (Grade 6 level) to more complex community-based ones (Grade 8 level); however, these levels are not prescriptive and teachers should choose activities according to students' needs and abilities.

Activities suitable for developing into assessment tasks include:

1. develop ways to be a wise consumer: draw up a budget, prepare a shopping list for materials required, compare prices and compare the qualities of different brands of commonly purchased items, discuss why students choose to shop in particular places and buy particular products, evaluate whether they get value for money
2. plan and carry out a project such as gardening, sewing or cooking
3. identify goods and services provided by local businesses and organisations
4. collect business documents, such as cash receipts, invoices and statements, from a range of organisations; display the documents and identify and explain the importance of the documents and the information on them
5. report on business strategies that provide quality services and satisfy customers
6. identify consumer problems—for example, overcrowded buses or stores, incorrect change, out-of-date products, dirty vehicles or premises, over-charging and damaged goods—and suggest strategies to minimise problems or seek redress
7. role-play returning a defective product to a store with a receipt of purchase.

Major links to other subjects

'Wise consumer' builds upon student learning in lower primary subjects, in particular Mathematics, Health and Community Living. At the upper primary level, 'wise consumer' has major links to the 'number and application' sub-strand of Mathematics, the 'changing roles and responsibilities' sub-strand in Personal Development, and the 'economic organisation' sub-strand in Social Science. These links are noted as icons in the student books.

Teacher information

Consumerism

We are all consumers. A consumer is a person who consumes or uses goods and services that are available.

Traditionally we consumed environmental products. We obtained our fish, meat, fruit, nuts and vegetables from the environment. We consumed bark, leaves and fibres for clothing, bags and baskets. We consumed bush timber for spears, shields, firewood, canoes and houses. Being a wise consumer meant being wise about how we used environmental products, taking only what we needed, and ensuring there would be supplies available for future generations.

In modern times, we tend to link the word 'consumerism' to goods and services that we purchase with money. Being a wise consumer in today's society means being wise about how we use our money so that we get value for the things we buy.

The importance of money

Money is important in today's society. We buy food, matches, toilet paper, soap, clothes and cooking pots from shops. We buy building materials and tools from timber yards and hardware shops. We pay for newspapers, books, pens, pencils, stamps and envelopes. We pay for education, health, telephone, electricity, water and garbage collection services. We pay to travel on vehicles, boats and aeroplanes. We buy cars, television sets, music systems and cassettes. We pay rent to live in houses that belong to other people. Wise consumers buy only what they can afford and avoid getting into debt through borrowing money.

From where do people get their money? Most people get money through the work they do to produce a product or service. Money that people get is called 'income'.

Some people are self-employed. They might grow vegetables, raise chickens or pigs, do carvings and make bilums to sell in markets. They might grow cash crops like coffee, tea, cocoa, rubber or vanilla and sell them to exporting companies. They might run a small business fixing tyres, run a trade store or operate a public motor vehicle (PMV) or boat service. Their income is not regular and may vary from week to week. To be successful, self-employed people need to have a product or service that people need or want, and that product or service must be of good enough quality to attract customers. This is also a focus of income-generating projects that students plan and do.

Some people get a salary by working for a government or private organisation. Their work could be as a driver, shop assistant, typist, mechanic, plumber, electrician, carpenter, manager, cleaner, lawyer, minister, priest, miner, security officer, salesperson, factory worker, nurse, doctor, teacher, clerk, inspector, police officer, judge, sailor or soldier. Their income is regular and does not vary from week to week, unless they are absent, get promoted or work overtime. To be successful, people who work for an organisation need to be competent at carrying out the duties required of them by their employer.

Some people get an income by letting other people use their land for roads, schools, hospitals, power pylons, mining, forestry, plantations, hotels, churches or other purposes. This form of income is usually a large amount that comes only once, although in some cases a smaller amount as an annual payment may be made. Compensation for land use is an issue in Papua New Guinea, with many landowners claiming that they were not paid sufficient money.

Money management

Budgets

An important concept for wise management of money is the concept of a budget. A budget is a plan for how expected income will be used. Individuals, families, businesses and governments all make budgets. Budgets are good because they show what the expected income is, what expenditures are planned and whether there will be something left over as savings or not enough money for planned expenses. A good personal or family budget is one where expenses do not exceed the expected income and there is something left over as savings for future unexpected or planned activities.

A business enterprise aims to make a profit. The profit is used to pay salaries, expand the business, improve services, and allow for depreciation on equipment or the purchase of new equipment. Imagine if you were to do a class project making frozen cordial in plastic cups. In Budget 1 shown in the table on page 47, a profit is shown. However, in Budget 2 we can see that the price of the cordial rose and no profit was made. What should you do? You could raise the selling price of the product.

You would also need to consider the replacement cost of a freezer or esky and whether your profit margin is large enough for this

Student for one week	Family for a fortnight
Expenses: exercise book K1.20, lunch for five days @ 50t a day K2.50, church money 20t = total K3.90 Income K5.00 Savings K1.10	Expenses: rent K35, utilities K50, food K200, entertainment K15, clothes K20, transport K20, household needs K40 = total K380.00 Income K400.00 Savings K20.00

Budget 1	Budget 2
Expenses: cordial K15, cups K6, electricity K3, water K1 = total K25.00. Expected income: 100 frozen cups of cordial at 30t each = K30.00. Profit K5.00	Expenses: cordial K20, cups K6, electricity K3, water K1 = total K30.00. Expected income: 100 frozen cups of cordial at 30t each = K30.00. Profit = nothing

expense in the future. Another consideration is that no allowance has been made for the labour costs. Making a profit of K5.00 on an outlay of K30.00 is a 16 per cent profit. In business a 30 per cent profit margin is acceptable. Keep this in mind as you budget and plan class income-generating projects.

As students consider income-generating projects that they can do in later life, the profit needs to cover a salary for living expenses for themselves or their family. A self-employed person needs to consider what their time and effort is worth in monetary terms. An hourly rate of K5.00 an hour for an eight-hour working day is equal to a weekly income of K200.00. The more skilled the labour, the higher the hourly rate would be.

Record-keeping

Wise consumers keep records. They may be personal records or business records. Records should be kept in a place that is clean and pest free to avoid damage. Records should be easy to retrieve when they are needed.

Examples of personal records are birth, death or marriage certificates; educational certificates as evidence of qualifications; and references as evidence of character or work performance. These records are useful for official purposes, gaining employment, getting travel visas or claiming allowances or benefits from employers.

Examples of business records are cash receipts, invoices and bank statements. When items are bought, the customer receives a handwritten or machine printed receipt. This shows what was bought, where it was bought and how much was paid. Should the item be defective, the customer may return the goods to the place of purchase and produce the receipt as proof of payment. The receipts are also useful for claiming reimbursements, transparency of payments being made and putting payments against budgeted expenses.

Records need to be kept for class income-generating projects. Financial documents indicate income, expenses and balance of money. They provide transparency and can be used to refute any claims of financial mismanagement. Other business records can be kept, such as a register of clients, duty roster for workers, dates when services are provided and different goods sold at various times. Records are valuable in assessing the success of a project.

Consumer rights, protection and responsibilities

Consumers have the right to expect that the products they are buying are safe and will not harm them. Food items should not cause illness. Kerosene lamps should not explode. Customers have a right to be informed about the contents of tins and packages and the price of goods on shelves. Customers have a right to be heard if they are dissatisfied with availability, cost or quality of goods and services. Customers have a right to return goods or be compensated if an item does not perform as it should. Customers have a right to a healthy environment in buses, shops and business premises. People have a right to consumer education to learn about good money management practices and hazards to avoid. Some 'fast money' schemes deceive people and result in customers losing their money.

The government has a responsibility to have laws to protect consumers. It controls what can and cannot be imported into the country. It controls the prices of some goods so that customers are not over-charged. Health inspectors can close down premises if cleanliness standards are low. Traffic departments control the issue of PMV licences to protect the safety of the travelling public. The public can lodge complaints with consumer affairs councils if they are dissatisfied with products or services.

Consumers also have responsibilities. They are responsible for critical awareness of what they are paying for and whether the price, service and value are satisfactory. They are responsible for taking appropriate action to be a wise consumer. They should make shopping lists, read labels, compare prices, check out the qualities of different brands, check that they are being charged accurately and receiving the right amount of change, ask for information or a demonstration before paying for equipment, keep records, return defective goods and complain if a service is unsatisfactory.

Suppliers

People have many needs and wants, and these are met by a range of organisations. Consumers generally value the organisations that provide the goods and services because they contribute to the quality of their lifestyle. If grandparents were to talk about the goods and services of long ago, it would be a different situation to what it is today. In earlier times, people were satisfied if they could get an axe, umbrella or metal cooking pot. Consumers of today, even those in remote rural areas, can access many consumer products and services that make life easier and more enjoyable.

Class projects

Choose projects from the list below that are appropriate for the school's local area and available resources. Set clear criteria for the satisfactory completion of tasks.

1. Visit local businesses and organisations that provide goods and services. Develop and use a set of criteria to assess the products and services. Listen to operators talk about the services they provide and strategies to provide quality services and satisfy customers.
2. Interview customers to get information about the type of problems they face—for example, overcrowded buses or stores, incorrect change, out-of-date products, dirty vehicles or premises, over-charging and damaged goods. Discuss strategies to minimise problems or seek redress.
3. Collect business documents such as cash receipts, invoices and statements from a range of organisations. Make a display of them. Identify and explain the importance of the documents and the information on them.
4. Plan and carry out an activity such as a gardening, sewing or cooking project. Apply ways to be a wise consumer. Draw up a budget. Prepare a shopping list for materials required. Compare prices and check out the qualities of different brands of commonly purchased items. Discuss why you choose to shop in particular places and buy particular products. Evaluate whether or not you get value for your money.
5. Obtain information on consumer rights and the laws that have been established to protect consumers. Role play returning a defective product to a store with a receipt of purchase.

SUB-STRAND 4 Making things

Main ideas

The main idea of the 'making things' sub-strand is for students to use a range of appropriate materials, tools, equipment and techniques to make things to benefit the individual or community. This includes recycled, craft, sewn, wood and metal items. Students are encouraged to be creative and are limited only by their imagination and the available resources as to what they can make. Learning reinforces pride and national identity in the production of home-made items.

The learning outcomes for 'making things' is shown in the following table:

Grade 6	Grade 7	Grade 8
6.2.4 Identify resources and a range of tools and equipment required for handcrafts and apply the skills in a familiar practical situation.	7.2.4 Initiate plans and apply appropriate techniques and processes to design and make an item that benefits the individual or the community.	8.2.4 Investigate the appropriateness of materials for specific purposes and use their imagination to design, make and evaluate a product relevant to their needs.

Key words

adaptation, aesthetic, carpentry, characteristics, construction, craftwork, design, flexibility, functional, handcrafts, initiative, innovation, originality, resources, scale drawings, sewing, specifications, technologies, texture, welding

Possible assessment tasks

Assessment aims to gather information on how well students achieve the learning outcomes for Sub-Strand 4 (Care and management). Clear criteria should be set for satisfactory completion of tasks.

The suggested activities are organised from simple school- or home-based activities (Grade 6 level) to more complex community-based ones (Grade 8 level); however, these levels are not prescriptive and teachers should choose activities according to students' needs and abilities.

Activities suitable for developing into assessment tasks include:

1. recycle materials such as aluminium cans, glass, cardboard, used fabric, paper, plastic containers, rice or flour bags to make useful things
2. sew household items such as curtains, cushion covers, pillowcases, bedcovers, tablemats, bags, handkerchiefs, hats
3. print T-shirts
4. create PNG designs on tea towels or babies' nappies, make placemats for table settings and tablecloths and sets of matching serviettes
5. make patterns for clothes, produce instruction sheets to make craft items, produce instruction sheets for furniture or metalwork household items
6. make clothes such as a skirt, shirt, blouse, dress and trousers; use stretch fabric; apply distinctive PNG designs; dye fabrics

Better Living

7 design uniforms for sports teams, women's groups, church choirs, music groups

8 weave holders for mobile phones, computer disks, drink cans or bottles

9 do craftwork such as making soft toys, baskets, mats, photo frames, carvings, walking sticks, ornaments, wall decorations, beads, armbands, ankle bands, hats, trays, woven placemats, candle holders, bilums, jewellery, spears, fishing nets, musical instruments, pencil holders

10 make things from wood such as a chopping board, coconut scraper, stool, chair, table, patrol box, pencil case, picture frame, bookshelf or cupboard

11 produce a metalwork product such as an oven tray, cooking plate or grill, tongs, strainer, grater, drum oven, garden rake, water tank.

Major links to other subjects

'Making things' builds upon student learning in lower primary subjects, in particular Art and Craft, Mathematics and Community Living. At the upper primary level, 'making things' has major links to the 'art' sub-strand of Arts, the 'measurement' and 'space and shape' sub-strands in Mathematics, and the 'culture' and 'environment and resources' sub-strands in Social Science. These links are noted as icons in the student books.

Teacher information

Making things

Markets, tourist shops and roadside stalls are evidence of the wonderful, uniquely Papua New Guinean things that people make to sell. In addition, a visit to a family home quickly reveals other marvellous ways in which people are making things for functional and aesthetic purposes in their homes.

Designs evolve as people experiment with different ways of doing things. Looking at a selection of bilums, we are constantly amazed by the construction techniques and variety of designs. The PNG flag, names and intricate patterns are blended together with a dazzling range of coloured yarns. Names and intricate patterns are also being incorporated into woven baskets and threaded into bands made of tiny beads. Clocks are being inserted into carvings where the clock is surrounded by carved crocodiles and Birds of Paradise. Personalised images are being transferred onto laplaps by printing or dyeing techniques. The creativity, initiative and innovative use of materials constantly amaze.

A large fuel drum can be cut in half, have an opening made on one side, and be upturned to become a stove. A large fuel drum can have one end cut off to become a door, have a shelf put inside and be turned into a drum oven. A large paint tin, with a small steel can in its side, can be filled with sawdust to become a sawdust stove. A small fuel drum with a round, stuffed cushion on top becomes a comfortable seat. Old tyres can be turned into playground equipment or safety barriers along edges of a waterfront. Old tyres can also be turned into pots for plants or used as borders on roads and gardens.

Usually, no one has formally taught people to do these things. People have a creative idea, see a need or useful purpose, dream up a design, make things from available resources, and experiment or modify original ideas until they are satisfied with the result. Sometimes the things are made for their own use and sometimes they are made to sell. This way of thinking and doing is what we are trying to encourage through Making a Living activities.

Having adequate resources for class projects could be an issue. It would be nice if parents provided resources or we had lots of money to buy materials from the shops to make things. In most schools in Papua New Guinea, this may not be the case. If you want to sell the goods you make, it will be important to survey the market to produce a product that appeals to and attracts customers. This is called finding a 'market niche'. Perhaps the Board of Management can allocate initial funds. Then it will be your responsibility to recycle the funds throughout the year with income from projects. Another approach is for students to provide the money or materials needed for something they will make. Generally, teachers and students will need to be inventive in identifying resources for making things.

Resources

Natural resources from our environment include bamboo, coconut shells, coconut husks, coconut fronds, trunks of coconut trees, bush ropes, bush fibres, pandanus, cane, clay, bark, pitpit, sago leaves, shells, nuts, seeds, kapok, driftwood, logs and bush timber. What other natural resources can you identify in your locality?

Resources purchased from stores include fabric, timber, plywood, plastic tubes, plastic sheeting, metal sheets, corrugated iron, metal rods, wire, glass panes, beads, threads, wool, nylon lines, string, rope, dowel rods, dyes, fabric printing inks, paints, varnishes, nails and cement. What other store-bought resources to make things with can you identify in your locality?

Waste products that can be recycled into useful items include tyres, sawdust, fuel drums, timber offcuts, metal roofing, old tanks, car bodies, paper, metal containers, glass bottles, scraps of fabric, old clothes, plastic pipes, plastic bags, plastic bottles, cartons, wooden crates, buckets, broken furniture, rubber tyre tubes, flour bags and rice bags. What other waste products that could be recycled can you identify in your locality?

Qualities of materials

Through handling and experimentation, students become familiar with the qualities of materials. Are they hard or soft? Are they flexible or rigid? Will they float or sink? Are they smooth or rough? Can they be moulded? Are they strong or weak? How would you join one piece to another? Can they be shaped, and if so, how? What colours are natural? What finishes can be applied?

Through observation, asking questions and brainstorming, many ideas can be generated about the qualities of materials for making things and their suitability for different items that can be made. For a barbecue plate or grill, the material needs to be fireproof so metal is more suitable than wood or plastic. Wood would burn; plastic would melt. For tongs or a stirring spoon, metal would conduct heat and burn the hand, so bamboo or wood would be more suitable.

Tools and equipment

The availability of tools will vary from school to school. A lack of tools should not be used as an excuse for not doing practical activities. Regard it as a challenge to be overcome.

Think of our ancestors and how they made axes, spears, shields, houses, ramps, boats, grass skirts, cooking and water containers, implements for preparing food, serving containers, clothing items, rain capes, items for decorating their houses, headdresses and all the other items they needed. What tools did they use? Maybe a class project could be to improvise and make tools to use. In this way you could develop a collection of improvised tools for making things.

Borrowing tools from the parents of the students could be an option. Involving parents in project activities might also be a way of encouraging them to share their tools with the class. Informing parents of the necessity of tools for Making a Living projects might lead to their putting pressure on the Board of Management to allocate funds for basic supplies.

The school needs to budget to provide a basic kit of equipment for Making a Living practical activities. These items are expensive. They need to be used appropriately to prevent unnecessary damage, maintained through appropriate care and stored securely when not in use. They are attractive items for dishonest people. Procedures are needed to prevent stealing. An assets register is needed to record items purchased. A record book should be maintained to record the borrowing and return of equipment. Tools will wear out through normal use and plans are needed to replace old and broken items.

Basic items for sewing activities include a sewing machine, needles, scissors, stitch unpicker, pins, tracing wheel and tape measure. The main consumable items are threads and fabric.

Basic items for woodwork activities include hammer, chisel, screwdrivers, ruler, clamp, plane, drill, drill bits, saw, mallet, sanding block and paintbrush. The main consumables are wood, nails, screws, glues, paint, varnish, sandpaper and solvent for cleaning brushes.

Basic tools for metalwork activities include steel rule, metal scriber, square, tin snips, hacksaw, file, pliers, hammer and mallet. The main consumables are sheet metal and wire.

Planning and designing items

Begin by investigating (a) the resources available to make things, (b) the types of handcrafts already being made, used or sold, (c) the properties of available materials and what they could be used for, (d) the tools and equipment available, (e) the expertise of the class teacher, other teachers, parents and other members of the local community and (f) sources of funding. Students can carry out investigations to identify needs of people and what they could make to meet those needs.

At a school level, collaborate with other teachers of Grades 6, 7 and 8 so that students acquire different skills over the years and make different items. Avoid repeating projects from one year to the next. An example is shown in the table below. However, the range of items being made could be much larger.

With students, begin by generating ideas through brainstorming. Your focus could be on a product or a particular type of material and how to use it.

- If bamboo is plentiful, the task could be to make something from bamboo. Brainstormed ideas could include eating utensils, cups, pencil holders, vases, room dividers, fences, seats, rafts, chairs, stools, picture frames, soap holders, cassette holders, candle holders, drums, musical instruments and napkin holders.
- If coconuts and coconut trees are plentiful, the task could be to make something from coconut. Brainstormed ideas could include brooms, hats, mats, fans, baskets, buttons, earrings, badges, eating utensils, cups, bowls on stands, money boxes, seats and bangles.
- If a targeted product was a mat, bag or basket, brainstormed ideas for materials could include fabric, recycled rice bag or flour bags, bush fibres, string, wool, pandanus or cane. Ideas for types of bag could include coin purse, shoulder bag, hand-held bag. Ideas for techniques could include sewing, weaving, interlocking loops, screen printing, tie dyeing.
- If a targeted product was jewellery or other form of personal adornment, brainstormed ideas could include hats, headdresses, headbands, wrist bands, anklets, necklaces. Ideas for materials could include shell, seeds, feathers, beads, pieces of coconut shell, pitpit, bamboo or flowers.
- If the targeted product was an item of clothing, brainstormed ideas could include tie-dyed

Grade 6	Grade 7	Grade 8
Natural resource: necklace, wristband	Natural resource: fan, comb	Natural resource: vase, pot plant, cup
Recycled resource: bag, basket, purse	Recycled resource: mat, photo frame	Recycled resource: pot plant, pencil container
Sewing: table mat, soft toy	Sewing: pillowcase, book bag	Sewing: sports shorts, skirt
Woodwork: pencil case, tray	Woodwork: book ends, bookshelf	Woodwork: stool, table
Metalwork: strainer, grater	Metalwork: cooking grill or oven tray	Metalwork: barbecue fork, coconut scraper

laplaps, screen printed T-shirts, sports shorts, school uniforms, blouses, skirts and trousers.

- If the targeted product was a sewn household item, brainstormed ideas could include pillowcases, curtains, bed covers, cushion covers, table cloths, table mats, napkins, curtain holders, tea-towels. Ideas for techniques could include tie-dyeing, screen printing, block printing or embroidery.

Once a focus has been achieved, students look at samples and think how designs can be imitated or adapted. The teacher should encourage creativity and diversity as much as possible. Students consider a range of design options and decide upon the most appropriate idea. Consideration is given to materials available, tools needed and skills involved. Individual project sheets are created that indicate the intended function of the item, the materials and tools that are needed, and the instructions to make the product.

If products are to be sold, consider targeted buyers, marketing strategies, costs, selling price, location and record-keeping. All products and processes should be evaluated to determine successes, constraints, suggested improvements and ideas for further projects.

Techniques and processes

Sewing techniques and processes include:

- designing clothes, choosing fabrics, making soft toys and household items
- taking body measurements, drafting patterns
- economically laying out pattern pieces onto fabric to minimise waste
- pinning and cutting
- using and maintaining sewing machine
- stitches (machine, tacking, running, backstitch, hemming)
- embroidery stitches (stem, satin, chain, blanket)
- seams (open, flat, French)
- darts, gathers, pleats
- hems
- collars, sleeves and pockets on clothing
- fastenings (zips, buttons, button holes, clip/snap fasteners, hooks and eyes, Velcro)
- mending (darning, patching, re-sewing seams, appliqué)
- colouring (screen and block printing, batik and tie-dyeing)

Craftwork techniques and processes include:

- designing, planning, choosing materials
- measuring, threading, weaving, plaiting, carving, knotting
- joining, gluing, sewing, drilling, nailing, hammering
- shaping, carving, cutting
- finishing, sandpapering, embroidery, painting, polishing, varnishing

Woodwork techniques and processes include:

- designing, planning, choosing suitable timber or wood
- measuring, sawing
- joining, nailing, screwing, gluing, drilling, hammering, planing
- shaping, bending, chiselling, sandpapering
- finishing, painting, polishing, varnishing

Metalwork techniques and processes include:

- designing, planning, choosing suitable types of metal

PROJECT SHEET

Project: Carved Turtle Dish

Use: For holding small things like coins or keys

Materials needed: a block of wood about 15 cm long, 10 cm wide and 5 cm thick, 2 small sea-shells for eyes

Tools needed: carving tools, sandpaper, glue, varnish, brush and solvent for cleaning the brush

Construction method: Shape the block of wood into a small turtle-shaped oval dish with a head at one end, a tail at the other and four legs. Hollow out areas where the two shells for eyes will be glued. Sand the surface until smooth. Glue in the eyes. Varnish all over to enhance the natural beauty of the wood grain.

Note: Clay could be used instead of wood to make the turtle dish.

- measuring, cutting
- joining, soldering, drilling
- shaping, grinding, bending
- finishing, painting

The value of appropriate technologies

An important aspect of technologies used to make things is that they are sustainable. Appropriate technologies have the following characteristics. They:

- are environmentally harmless
- build on locally understood technologies
- can be understood, controlled and maintained by people without a high level of education
- involve local people, ideally responding to a real need
- minimise the need for people to move away from traditional communities
- offer opportunities for further employment and economic activity
- provide a competitive product or service
- provide a product or service of acceptable quality, with high reliability, low maintenance and ease of access
- provide opportunities for benefits to the people as a whole rather than a privileged group
- provide work satisfaction
- require affordable maintenance
- require low capital investment per workplace
- use existing or easily adaptable skills with minimum retraining
- use local materials and energy
- use proven techniques, to reduce the possibility of failure

Class projects

1 Investigate sources of materials that can be recycled. Design and make a product from recycled material. This could be a carry bag from a rice bag; a flower vase from a tin or glass jar; a plant holder, swing or climbing frame from old tyres; a child's pair of shorts from an old laplap; a seat or table top from a section of fallen log; a cassava grater made by punching nail holes in a piece of sheet metal; an oven or stove from a fuel drum.

2 Identify local resources that can be used for handcrafts, such as cane, clay, bamboo, bush fibres, timber offcuts, coconut leaves, coconut shells, pandanus, shells and nuts. Design and make a product from local resources. Creativity, uniqueness, a national identity, usefulness and appeal are encouraged. Items could be hats, brooms, drums, fans, mats, bilums, jewellery, carvings, headbands, dishes, chairs, trays, armbands, ankle bands, baskets, photo frames, toys or room dividers. Evaluate what you have done, examining the benefits and costs in functional, aesthetic and environmental terms.

3 Visit shops and hardware stores to observe and price a range of materials that can be bought to make things. This could include fabric, wool, nylon string, beads, plywood, milled timber, plastic pipes, sheets of plastic, sheet metal, steel rods, corrugated iron and dowel rods. Develop skills in appropriate construction techniques and use of tools. Make economical use of materials to plan and make things for specific purposes, such as furniture, gardening, clothing, cooking, entertainment, fishing, hunting and building extensions.

4 Plan a display of finished products and present them for sale. Assess suitability of the texture, flexibility, strength, smoothness, shape and colour of the materials for the chosen product. Calculate costs, determine selling price and present for sale at suitable times in appropriate locations. Maintain records.

STRAND 3

Community Development

About this strand

In the Community Development strand, students use the Making a Living process skills of 'investigation, planning and designing, making or producing, marketing or using, evaluating' to learn new ideas, knowledge, skills and attitudes on how to contribute to, live and work within their local community. Students learn the necessary skills to become aware of their community's needs and to assist in making improvements by planning and implementing community development projects relevant to the community. They also develop their potential as useful and valued community members by:

- raising awareness about available community resources
- sourcing assistance from NGOs to develop essential community projects
- helping to make democratic decision-making processes that benefit the community

This strand consists of three sub-strands:

- knowing your communities
- communication
- community projects

Key concepts that teachers need to develop in all activities are:

- relationships
- public relations
- social and economic development

There is one learning outcome for each sub-strand for each grade. The learning outcomes are broad and can be achieved in any context depending on available resources and expertise. Elaborating on the learning outcomes generates ideas that help the teacher to identify content and activities, possible projects and assessment tasks. From the learning outcome elaborations, teachers can write units of work and teaching programs suited to local conditions, available resources and expertise.

The following is a sample elaboration of the Grade 6 learning outcome. The ideas are not exhaustive and teachers are encouraged to develop their own.

Example of elaborating a learning outcome

Grade: 6

Strand: Community Development

Sub-strand: Knowing your communities

Learning outcome: *6.3.1. Identify the common features of the local community and make suggestions as to how this may influence or benefit community life.*

Community Development

Two key areas can be derived from this outcome: features of a community and how features benefit community life. Each area can be elaborated.

For example, the area of community services can be elaborated in the following ways:

- Transport—This would include the making of roads and bridges as well as transportation vehicles such as PMV buses, private cars, canoes, outboard motors, planes, bicycles. Develop this further to look at costs associated with transport modes and maintenance of transport vehicles.
- Water supply—This can be developed into ways of keeping water safe for drinking, cooking and laundry, and ways of keeping water clean from water diseases. Investigate water systems that supply water to the community (for example, pipes, tanks, wells, bore wells, creeks). How can these systems be improved as the population grows?
- Health services—aid posts, health centre, clinics and hospitals, traditional herbal clinics. Investigate how these function and the costs associated with each centre.

From the ideas generated, the teacher can then decide on the topics that are most appropriate to develop, taking into account students' prior knowledge as well as the resources and expertise available.

The *time allocation* for Making a Living is 360 minutes per week. This allows time for practical activities so that students can get out of the classroom to investigate and gather information. An example is shown in the following table:

Monday	Tuesday	Wednesday	Thursday	Friday
9am–12am Visit the local health centre and listen to a health worker talk about health services offered at the centre. 1pm–2pm Write a report on the services offered at the centre and how to improve centre services.		9am–12am Visit the health centre again and carry out jobs either to improve the appearance of the building and surrounds (e.g., cutting grass, cleaning the grounds, planting trees or flowers) or to improve hygiene standards inside the centre (e.g., washing floors, walls).		9am–10am Draw posters that relay the message ***We need to look after our community health centre*** and post on the community notice board.

Assessment is an ongoing process and should be carried out as students undertake activities. Possible assessment ideas for the above example could include:

- interview health workers to find out the major challenges facing the health centre
- write letters to the Health Department asking for specific equipment or financial support for the health centre
- plan and carry out community work to improve conditions at the health centre

SUB-STRAND 1 # Knowing your communities

Main ideas

The main idea of the 'knowing your communities' sub-strand is for students to gain knowledge about their community, the major features of their community and how their community is organised. The learning outcomes for each upper primary grade for 'knowing your communities' are shown in the following table:

Grade 6	Grade 7	Grade 8
6.3.1 Identify the common features of their local community and make suggestions as to how these may influence or benefit community life.	7.3.1 Reflect upon their personal strengths and capabilities and consider how they might use these to contribute in a positive way within the community.	8.3.1 Apply an understanding of the local community to develop and undertake a cooperative plan that provides economic and social opportunities and benefits for their community.

Key words

features, transport, location, climate, population, services, interaction, sustainable, culture, public relations, self-reliance, self-esteem, community, conservation, environment

Possible assessment tasks

Assessment aims to gather information on how well students achieve the learning outcomes for 'Knowing your community'. Clear criteria should be set for satisfactory completion of tasks.

The suggested activities are organised from simple school- or home-based activities (Grade 6 level) to more complex community-based ones (Grade 8 level); however, these levels are not prescriptive and teachers should choose activities according to students' needs and abilities.

Activities suitable for developing into assessment tasks include:

1. plan and conduct a cultural day, school fete or open day
2. repair, clean and polish shoes; make footwear
3. provide labour for child-minding services
4. help sick or disabled people
5. conduct classes for people who cannot read or write
6. hold celebrations for special events such as World Environment Day, Book Week, Mothers' Day, Fathers' Day, Easter, Christmas, Independence Day, Remembrance Day
7. organise a public meeting to discuss specific social problems in the community, such as land shortages; settlement issues; tribal fights; movement from rural to urban areas; or better services for health, education or transport
8. suggest possible community improvements such as a new marketplace, a rubbish-collection service, solar-powered lighting and heating, clean water supplies

Major links to other subjects

'Knowing your communities' builds upon student learning in lower primary subjects, in particular Community Living. At the upper primary level, 'knowing your communities' has major links to the substrands 'people and environment' and 'social and economic organisation' of Social Science and to the substrands of 'interactions in relationships and groups' and 'cultural and personal identity' of Personal Development. These links are noted as icons in the student books.

Teacher information

Features of a community

'Location' means the land where a community settles. The location of a settlement depends on the local environment. Geographic location has some influence on family and population sizes throughout Papua New Guinea. Teachers and students can compare their location with others and identify its benefits, describe why the location has been chosen for settlement, and investigate the systems and practices that are in place for community members to support one another in times of natural disasters. Students can discuss factors that make it difficult for important government services to reach rural and isolated communities.

Topics that can be developed into units of work include:

Location:

- garden land—soil composition, current gardening practices, crop harvesting, crop sustainability practices
- water supply—type of supply, accessibility, clean water issues, sustainability for a growing population
- transport—access to roads or rivers, how the issue of transport affects the development of a community (for example, getting produce to market)

Climate:

- major features
- types of houses that are built to adjust to climate, type of materials used
- food that is grown, cash crops

Natural resources:

- food supply from hunting and gathering, how forest resources are used by the community economically, culturally and medicinally
- types of building structures, building materials and their uses

Population:

- numbers of people, effects on the community—economically (for example, in housing, food supply, basic services) and socially (for example, land disputes, law and order, unemployment)
- land development, land clearance, loss of natural resources, economic and ecological issues

Culture:

- local traditions and rituals—what they mean, how they are practised and passed on
- values—the effects of changing values as a community becomes more sophisticated

Services. A community has specific needs and wants in terms of services. There are three main types:

- *Government services* such as health, water, power, education, protection (police, army), mail, telecommunications. These services are funded by money collected from people in the community through rates and taxes.
- *Community services* such as St John Ambulance, Red Cross, sports groups, YWCA, churches. These services are generally provided by church groups and other organisations. They are usually free to the public.

- *Commercial services* such as entertainment, petrol, air travel, banking, newspapers, shipping, market selling. These services are provided by private businesses, and people pay for the services or the goods they are buying.

Each of these areas can be elaborated. For example, the area of population can be elaborated into population growth and increase; causes of population increase (such as better health and nutrition, low infant deaths, immunisation programs, increased life span); and social problems related to population increase (such as unemployment, crime, land shortage, overcrowding and population imbalance in rural and urban areas).

Relationships between school and community

The community has a responsibility to the school because the school belongs to the community. The community needs to support the school by providing services when a need arises. This will help teachers run the school properly. The community needs to work together with the primary school head teacher, the teachers and the board of management, to work out how best they can support the primary school.

The school also needs to build relationships with the community. This can be best achieved by:

- listening and observing people within the local community
- identifying the people who make things happen, the leaders, both male and female
- asking questions about ways the community is organised for decision-making and what processes need to be followed
- finding out about the main issues for different groups of people. The community will be made up of various groups, each with its own interests, agendas and needs
- spending time with different groups—meeting the parents out of school and getting to know the children in their own backgrounds
- visiting different groups—not waiting for them to come to the school
- making a list of all different community resources, including:
  - ➢ places to visit
  - ➢ people who can share skills and knowledge
  - ➢ environmental resources
  - ➢ technical schools, museums, gardens and other community businesses
- making contacts and building up a network of resource people. These could include other teachers, NGOs, public servants, health workers, women's organisations

Ways in which the local community can assist a school include:

- supporting children by showing an interest in their school's work
- building functional buildings (these can be bush material buildings) for practical lessons such as those in Making a Living
- providing land where possible for agriculture projects
- helping teach the children community skills and knowledge, such as fishing, net maintenance, weaving, cooking, gardening, sewing, and modern skills such as animal farming and carpentry
- raising funds so the school can purchase essential teaching items
- volunteering to maintain buildings and other facilities in the school

Personal strengths and capabilities

By discussing individual strengths and capabilities, students can assess what each individual is good at doing and how this is important within a community. For example, some people may be good at gardening and managing cash cropping while others have good public relations or building skills.

Skills such as good sports capabilities, problem-solving, academic skills, public relations, interpersonal skills and technical skills can allow community members to volunteer their time, labour and resources to contribute to community development. Young people need to understand and appreciate the fact that their education and training should equip them with skills and knowledge that they can use to improve the living standard of their community. This should lead them to understand the importance of working within the community, which in turn will gain them respect from the community. Trust is then built within the community and good working relationships are established, thus leading to self-reliance.

When students reflect on their strengths and capabilities or those of other members of the community, they can:

- share life experiences by developing personal profiles or making oral presentations
- swap their profiles with others and study someone else's profile to identify strengths and capabilities
- invite successful business people, pastors, hunters, chicken farmers, carvers, sports personalities and others in the community to speak to them about how they have used their skills and personal attributes to contribute to the community

Using a school's combined strengths and capabilities, the school can undertake a variety of activities that benefit not only the school but also the local community. On health issues, for example, students could develop an awareness of the importance of nutrition and compose a nutrition song to sing, or perform role-plays on nutrition related themes. In terms of community economic projects, they could develop a project proposal to establish or maintain a water supply, establish a school food garden using different introduced farming techniques (invite community members to take part in this project), or help construct a 'resting haus' or a market for selling of market foods.

By contributing to the community's well-being, people

- gain respect from the community and improve their self-image. This makes community members value and appreciate help from others.
- build trust and good working relationships. This makes people want to live and work together in peace and enjoy the company of others.
- promote self-reliance, using locally available resources to cater for all the needs of the community.
- improve the living standard in the community. This leads to better nutrition, longer lifespan, good and healthy homes, clean water for drinking and cooking and so on.

Understanding and knowledge of the local community

Students need to understand and develop deep knowledge about the communities they come from. They do this by looking at the culture, traditions and important values of these communities, and at how many of these are being replaced by new changes brought on by modern ideas and influences.

In Papua New Guinea culture is still strong, and there are many differences in the culture of people from different parts of the country. For example, the way people make houses and gardens varies from province to province. Other differences include customs (such as bride price), beliefs (spirits, sorcery, magic), traditions (items such as bilums, pottery, weaving, carving) and ceremonies (initiation of young people, marriage).

Students need to understand their local culture, traditions and values, what these mean and how they are practised and passed on from generation to generation. They also need to consider how traditional culture is changing and the effects of this change, both positive and negative.

Families are important in all communities. Students need to examine different types of families (nuclear and extended) and how they operate within a community. Other family related issues include clan loyalties, the wantok system and networks. Consider these family systems in the light of modern development.

Population growth and control is also very important. How does a community meet the basic needs of a growing population? How can it tackle the associated social problems including land disputes, migration and tribal fights?

Geographic location (for example, coastal, highlands) is another influence on the character of a community. So is the availability of natural resources. The development of natural resources brings benefits to the community. Land and water resources (sea, gardens, forests, rivers, lakes, minerals) are important resources for meeting community needs.

Students can also examine how community development can influence and benefit the community in terms of the establishment of schools, health centres, PMV services, churches, clean water supplies and rural electricity supply. Opportunities for money-making activities give community members a chance to take part in economic development projects in both the formal and informal sectors (for example, selling ice blocks, polishing shoes, growing and selling cash crops, working in a store).

Sustainable development practice

There is a need to practise ways of using natural resources that conserve those resources for future generations. Sustainable development refers to changes that can be sustained or maintained for continued growth and improvement within society. Not all development leads to a better life for the people.

Changes and development in Papua New Guinea have had an enormous impact on people in every aspect of life. Some of these changes are economic, such as the setting up of large industries like cash crop plantations and large-scale mining activities. Some changes are social, such as the movement of people from the country to towns and cities in search of a better lifestyle and employment. Some changes are ecological and environmental—the effects of large-scale development can cause many problems if it is not regulated, including pollution, destruction of habitats and environmental degradation.

Class projects

Choose projects from the list below that are appropriate for the school's local area and available resources. Set clear criteria for the satisfactory completion of tasks.

1 Plan an excursion to walk around the local community. Observe and record its features. Draw a community resources map identifying the major features. Conduct a survey or interview members of the community on how these features influence or benefit the community. Make suggestions on how these features can be developed to improve the lives of people in the community.

2 Draw a diagram of your school's water supply system. Suggest possible improvements.

3 Measure and draw a map of your school area and record all major features. Suggest one small project to improve your school grounds and buildings.

4 Conduct a school population census.

5 Plan an activity for a cultural day for your school, a school fete or an open day.

6 Organise a public meeting to discuss specific social problems relating to the community, such as land shortages, settlement issues, tribal fights or rural-to-urban movement.

Community Development

These sample class projects show how to match activities with process skills, and identify teaching strategies, assessment tasks and materials.

SAMPLE PROJECT: Market shelves

Market shelves are used for food display in marketplaces in schools or in local communities and towns. Having market food and items displayed on the shelves is better than having food displayed on the ground, which is unhygienic. Shelves are made at waist height to be convenient for the buyer and for the seller to stand or sit comfortably when marketing.

Materials

- saplings/timbers
- strings
- nails
- plywood or smoothed wood

Tools

- saw
- claw hammer
- nails, digging tool (spade)
- axe, knives

Steps for construction

1. Select site, then clear and dig hole for post and frame.
2. Following project sketch/plan, set up frame and cover holes with small stones and soil to make frame firm (use cement if you have it).
3. Make shelves using the wood saplings or timber and nail to fasten.
4. Nail plywood or smoothed wood/palms to provide a surface on which market items can be placed.
5. Seats can be made next to the market shelves. Shelters can be built for shade.
6. The shelves are now ready for use by vendors.

SAMPLE PROJECT UNIT: Community Resource Mapping

Grade: 6

Strand: Community Development

Sub-strand: Knowing your communities

Learning outcome: *6.3.1. Identify the common features of the local community and make suggestions as to how this may influence or benefit community life.*

Purpose: The purpose of this unit is to allow students to survey the community and draw a resource map of the community to identify common features. This can be used as a reference to discuss benefits and make suggestions for possible improvements.

Unit Content

Knowledge	Skills	Attitudes
Students demonstrate an understanding of: • common community features • a resources map to identify, plan and carry out a project to promote community resources • natural and built-up resources, with their benefits	Students develop the skills to: • use symbols and keys correctly on maps representing the resources of the community • be more observant about resources in the community • neat and accurate record-keeping	Students develop attitudes: • the value of resources and their sustainable use • appreciating records such as a resource map • developing a project to benefit the school or village community

Overview of teaching and learning activities

Process skills	Teaching and learning strategies		Materials
Investigation	• identify the geographical location • observe and make mental notes of the features • survey and note the location of the resources	discussion excursion brainstorming	sketch paper pencils rubber/eraser
Planning and design	• choose suitable scale and key for the map • sketch out the map • make drafts for suggestions and review	discussions creative thinking group work	drawing materials paper (A4 size) pencils
Making or producing	• develop mapping skills to include resources in the correct proportion • apply appropriate mapping techniques • produce results of high quality which can be referenced	modelling trailing creative thinking	drawing materials
Marketing or using	• share information with others • use the map to plan and carry out projects using available resources • store away for later reference	discussions group work brainstorming creative thinking	staplers drawing pins folders
Evaluating	• identify successes, failures and constraints • determine whether the project met the intended outcome • suggestion adaptations to improve	reflection critique discussions	writing materials

SUB-STRAND 2 Communication

Main ideas

The main ideas of the 'communication' sub-strand are for students to learn how to use written and oral communication methods, develop communication skills through using oral, print and electronic means, and use these skills to establish networking partners. Students learn that public relations and promoting awareness of important community issues such as HIV/AIDS, nutrition and adult literacy can use these communication skills.

The learning outcomes for each upper primary grade for 'communication' are shown in the following table:

Grade 6	Grade 7	Grade 8
6.3.2 Investigate and practise practical skills of effective communication.	7.3.2 Identify and establish network partners within the wider community to promote more effective access to information.	8.3.2 Apply effective communication skills and mediums to facilitate awareness of an issue of concern to the community.

Key words

information, literacy, networking, participation, medium, interview, relationship, technology, contacts, communication, telephone, Internet, computer, issues, postal services

Possible assessment tasks

Assessment aims to gather information on how well students achieve the learning outcomes for Sub-strand 2 (Communication). Clear criteria should be set for satisfactory completion of tasks.

The suggested activities are organised from simple school- or home-based activities (Grade 6 level) to more complex community-based ones (Grade 8 level); however, these levels are not prescriptive and teachers should choose activities according to students' needs and abilities.

Activities suitable for developing into assessment tasks include:

1. produce writing paper and envelopes with a PNG image
2. produce a class or school newsletter in Tokples, Tok Pisin and/or English
3. design a poster on a community issue or to advertise an event, conduct a public awareness campaign
4. write reports for publication in national newspapers or to be reported on a local radio station, write letters to editors of national newspapers
5. read newspapers, listen to the radio, watch television, write letters, use a computer, send a fax, use a telephone, visit a radio station
6. conduct an interview
7. produce a drama to perform to the community about issues such as conservation, wise use of water, unwanted pregnancies, domestic violence, school fee payments, safety when travelling in boats or vehicles, working with people with disabilities
8. organise a seminar, forum or discussion group on an issue such as elections, raskol activities, eviction of settlers, activities of foreign investors, mining, logging, fishing

Major links to other subjects

The 'communication' sub-strand builds upon student learning in the lower primary subject, in particular Community Living. At the upper primary level, 'communication' has major links to the sub-strand 'social and economic organisation' of Social Science, the substrand 'making choices' of Personal Development and the substrand skills and strategies of Language. These links are noted as icons in the student books.

Teacher information

Following are elaborations of the key areas in the 'communication' sub-strand. The lists are not exhaustive and teachers are encouraged to add to them. Teachers should choose ideas that are relevant to their students and locations and elaborate further to develop project units of work and assessment tasks.

The importance of effective communication

- **Keeping the community informed.** This means sharing information and promoting awareness on issues of concern in the community.

- **Meeting other people.** This gives confidence and self-esteem to individuals and groups. It would include conducting interviews and learning proper listening and speaking techniques.
- **Maintaining good relationships in the community.** Invite community members, networking partners such as village elders, skilled people, government officers and community workers to the school to give speeches or promote awareness.

The importance of relationships

Building relationships is a two-way process. Each of us has responsibilities and roles which carry expectations. The following guide serves to reinforce the expectations and responsibilities we have as individuals towards our school or community:

- What kind of community do I live in?
- Who are the key people (both formal and informal) in my community?
- Who has the most power in my community?
- Who are the people who get things done?
- The need to collect organisational information—meeting dates, calendars, plans
- The need to continually update information

The importance of networking

Promoting networking includes working cooperatively with village elders, community workers, church groups, NGOs and government officers. Networking is communication between groups for sharing information, contacts and other resources.

Networking is based on human contact between individuals and groups. This need not necessarily be face-to-face. It can also be through letters, fax machines, cassettes, telephones or email.

Networking is reciprocal—that is, it is a mutual relationship where both parties give and take. In networking, people should involve all their contacts in giving and receiving information to ensure all information is made available to as many as possible. To file away useful information and communication is against the process and principles of networking.

Communication mediums

Major communication mediums in Papua New Guinea are word of mouth, radio, newspapers, telephone, mail, television and electronic media, including fax and email.

Radio

Papua New Guinea has a large radio network that transmits information to all parts of the country in many languages. Schools use radio programs in their teaching and most students have access to a radio in their village. The National Broadcasting Commission (NBC) is the only radio broadcasting authority in the country. It provides radio services to about four million people. The NBC is made up of three networks:

Karai is the national service which transmits on both medium wave and short wave frequencies.

Kundu is the network responsible for fourteen provincial radio stations throughout the country. All these stations broadcast on short wave frequencies.

Kalang is the commercial arm of NBC, which broadcasts on an FM band. It is made up of fifteen relay stations throughout the country. It sells airtime and operates independently as a business-oriented radio station.

Three main languages commonly used in Papua New Guinea are the main broadcast languages— Tok Pisin, Hiri Motu and English. However, the provincial stations under the Kundu network use several vernacular languages from particular areas in their locations. The nineteen provincial stations between them use about sixty languages to broadcast as well as the three national languages.

Newspapers

Newspapers are very scarce outside Port Moresby and other major cities. However, some communities produce local newssheets that inform people with news regarding the local area. Although newspapers are readily available in the larger cities, not all people read them regularly as they cannot afford to purchase a daily paper.

Newspapers are an excellent resource for teachers to gain up-to-date information on current political, economic, social or environmental issues.

PNG Post Courier—daily newspaper, English
The National—daily newspaper, English
Times of PNG—weekly newspaper, English
Wantok Niuspepa—weekly newspaper, Tok Pisin
PNG Business—monthly specialist business newspaper, English
Hiri-Nius—monthly newspaper covering national government news, English, Tok Pisin and Hiri Motu
Eastern Star—provincial fortnightly newspaper in Milne Bay Province, English
Madang Watcher—provincial monthly newspaper covering Sepik and Morobe news, English, Tok Pisin

Television and electronic media

There is one local television station, EM TV: Media Niugini Pty Ltd. Rural areas have no broadcast television services. Videos are becoming available and are used for recreational purposes. Computers are being used in major cities and the use of email as a communication medium is growing, but only in the major cities.

Effective communication skills

Effective communication skills include speaking, listening, reading and writing.

Speaking and listening are important skills if people are to function as a group. Effective listening skills include reading gestures, eye contact and interviewing. Some good listening techniques include the following:

Type of listening technique	Purpose	Possible responses from a good listener
Listening for clarity	to get further information or to help in understanding the problem	'Can you clarify this?' 'Do you mean this?' 'Is this the problem as you see it now?'
Listening for restatement	to check meaning and interpretation	'Do you mean this?' 'Is this the problem as you see it now?'
Attentive listening	to show you are interested and wish the speaker to keep speaking	'I see.' 'That's a good point.'
Reflective listening	to show you understand what the speaker feels to help you evaluate what has been said	'You felt that you didn't get a fair hearing.' 'You feel that…'
Summarising listening	to summarise the speaker's thoughts	'I feel that you expressed these key ideas—do you agree?'

Reading is a communication skill because when we read we gain certain information. This information we may use to improve our knowledge and skills. We may pass on information that affects our community economically, socially or environmentally. We may also read purely for pleasure. The mediums for reading include newssheets, newspapers, pamphlets, magazines, posters and books.

Writing is another communication skill. When we write, we write for a purpose. This may be related to our work or to our personal lives. The different writing forms include letters (formal and informal), reports, school assignments, examination tests, stories, plays, newsletters.

Collecting data and information requires the

use of reading and writing skills. Some ways data is collected and collated include questionnaires, interviews, surveys, censuses, tables, graphs.

Identifying network partners

There are many groups that can assist the school community to provide better facilities and resources for the school. They range from government departments to small informal community groups. It is important to identify possible network partners for your area and find out how they are able to assist in current school projects.

Possible network partners include:

Government officers—This includes health workers (nurses, health extension officers), teachers, ol didiman/ol meri, police officers and district managers and other government workers that are network partners in community development.

Non-government groups—Non-government organisations are often set up with support from overseas agencies such as World Wide Fund for Nature (WWF), Volunteer Service Overseas (VSO), World Vision, Save the Children Fund and other community-based groups.

Churches—Church-related network partners may include church youth groups, church welfare groups and church-run schools, health services, and social and spiritual human development services.

Community elders and specialists—This includes village elders and traditional arts and crafts people who possess valuable skills and talents to share with students.

Local level governments—This includes local level government officers such as local level councillors and district administrative officers, who form an important communication network in the community.

Business community—This includes business groups that operate in the community, district and province such as local village business groups or associations, Public Motor Vehicle (PMV) operators, trade store owners, businessmen and businesswomen, all of whom also form an important network for community development.

Establishing contact with network partners

In order to establish contact and working relationships with network partners we need the following skills and qualities:

- **Ability to communicate.** Know all about your school and how it works, and be able to impart this information to potential partners.
- **Trustworthiness.** Be reliable. Provide good information. Do not create expectations that you cannot meet.
- **Professionalism.** Take time to listen carefully. Be interested in the people you deal with. Do not waste people's time. Know when and how to say no. Be cooperative and see yourself as part of a team. Stay focused on the main goal.
- **Ability to solve problems.** Do not react too quickly. Gather the necessary information before reacting. Deliver bad news personally. Seek help when necessary. Have alternative strategies prepared.

Some ways of building and establishing a relationship with network partners would include:

- Make initial contacts with partner organisations. This can be done through workshops, meetings, fellowships, sports meetings, school P&C meetings. Contacts can also be made through writing letters, sending fax messages, making telephone calls or meeting people face to face.
- Organise meetings. This may mean planning and organising a community meeting to gather information and ideas or to promote awareness and gain support for the community or school development. It can be done through school P&C meetings, local councillors' community meetings, church meetings.
- Use the telephone as a fast medium of communication. When making telephone calls, proper manners and how to use the telephone must be learned.

- Write a letter. This can be a personal letter or a business letter. When writing business letters, the correct format and layout must be followed.

Some network partners may be NGOs. The term 'NGO' stands for Non-Government Organisation, and was first used in 1995 in the UN charter. Today it is commonly used for any organisation that is not from the government or the business world. Some NGOs have been set up specifically to work in Papua New Guinea and operate nationally, such as the National Volunteer Service (NVS). Others are regional or local providers, such as the Sepik Council of Women (ESCOW).

Many NGOs are international organisations with offices in various countries including Papua New Guinea. Volunteer Services Overseas (VSO), Save the Children Fund (SCF) and World Wide Fund for Nature (WWF) are three examples. There are other names for different types of NGOs which you may come across, such as CBO (Community Based Organisation). CBOs are usually small organisations dedicated to a particular issue or service. Examples include youth and church groups.

NGOs are often set up to provide services in communities where governments do not or cannot operate. Providing health care in isolated communities and managing marine life in Milne Bay Province are examples. Features of NGOs include:

- non-bureaucratic
- flexible and often responsive to change and local needs
- grassroots and often poorly funded
- often funded to work in specific areas of development

Effective communication skills

Raising issues of community concern

There are many issues of concern to the community that need to be addressed by utilising effective communication skills.

One important example is land disputes. This includes disputes over customary land boundaries and traditional ownership of land, squatter settlement problems faced in urban areas, and the associated problems of squatter settlement eviction exercises. Tribal fights and land compensation demands are the result of land disputes. Land disputes hinder development progress in communities and in the nation as a whole. Well-informed communication within communities can solve this problem.

The problem of law and order can also badly affect the community and economic development of a nation. Law and order issues include rascalism (caused mostly by unemployed youths), rape, drugs, tribal fighting and the negative attitudes of people. Effective communication carried out at the community level in partnership with network partners would help solve the law and order problem in our communities, schools and the nation.

Literacy

Communication also helps with literacy and health. Being able to read and write helps people to live a healthy life. Literate communities can keep themselves informed by reading newspapers, can carry out awareness campaigns on economic, social and environmental issues affecting communities, and can keep themselves and their surroundings clean and healthy.

Education

Education requires communication. Education means not only being literate but learning the skills, values and attitudes that are needed to be a productive and useful member of the community. Learning can be formal or informal (such as fishing, weaving a basket, gardening and hunting).

Why communication skills are important

Effective communication skills can be used to:

- keep the community informed about happenings and issues affecting them such as health, nutrition, farming, marketing, local and world news. Communication mediums include newspapers, community notice boards, television programs, radio, meetings to help improve their lifestyle.

- meet other people within and outside of your community and relate well with them. This includes social skills such as greeting people, being respectful, polite and friendly, and developing positive attitudes acceptable to people.
- maintain good relationships in the community, sharing information, understanding and respect for each others' views. Positive qualities such as politeness, kindness, tolerance, loving and caring are the essence that ensures a peaceful atmosphere and environment in the community.
- promote networking, including building good relationships with network partners. Making contacts and maintaining good relations enable people to share resources, information, skills and ideas to develop our communities.

Using communication to facilitate awareness can be elaborated into:

- Use a range of communication mediums, including newspapers, radios, fax, email, letters, the Internet, computer, television, telephones. These communication mediums ensure that the community within and abroad is well-informed of happenings and issues affecting the community and nation. These mediums contribute to community development.
- Use effective communication skills. This includes oral communication skills such as speaking and listening skills; gestures and good eye contact; writing skills such as writing business or formal letters; and other skills necessary to ensure effective communication.
- Promote a participatory approach. This means getting the community involved in making decisions about community development projects, participating in the projects, having ownership of the projects and maintaining the projects. The communication skills of listening are vital, so that everyone's views and opinions are expressed and decisions are made collaboratively.

Class projects

Choose projects from the list below that are appropriate for the school's local area and available resources. Set clear criteria for the satisfactory completion of tasks.

1 Sketch the organisational structure of your school and community. Use symbols to represent and explain the relationships that exist between different levels.

2 Discuss ways you could get community people to build relationships with your school. Think of ways you could get these people interested in your school and what skills each group could share with your school.

Group/person	How they can assist the school	Skills available/needed
parents		
community elders		
health workers		
local artists		
local NGOs		
local businesses		
government officers		
others		

Community Development

3 Write a letter on behalf of your local community to attract the interest of a potential donor. You may wish to use this format:

Your address ....

....

Date ....

Person's name ....

Organisation ....

Address ....

Dear ....

Your name was given to me by .... and I understand that you offer help to groups in Papua New Guinea with .... projects.

I am a member of .... We are planning to start a project to .... Our group will need help with ....

We know a little about your organisation but would like to know more. Would it be possible for a representative from your organisation to visit .... so that we can explain our project more fully? Hopefully, you may be interested in helping us with this project.

I enclose our project proposal with this letter. We are happy to supply any further information that you may require regarding this proposal.

If your organisation cannot assist us, can you suggest another organisation that may be able to help?

Yours sincerely,

....

4 Write a project proposal on behalf of your community to attach to this letter. In this proposal you need to state:

- the project objective
- the project implementation plan
- the project costs and required resources
- the project time frame
- the project evaluation

5 Relationships between people in the village can be very complex. Use diagrams to show the interrelationship between clans and organisations.

6 The wantok system has been a traditional form of relationship between people for a long time. The traditional wantok system was based on reciprocity (that is, it was a two-way system). Interview people in your community to find out how the wantok system works now. Present your findings as an oral report during an Open Day at your school.

This sample class project shows how to match activities with process skills, and identify teaching strategies, assessment tasks and materials.

SAMPLE CLASS PROJECT: Producing a School Newsletter

Grade: 6

Strand: Community Development

Sub-strand: Communication

Learning outcome: *6.3.2 Investigate and practise practical skills of effective communication.*

Purpose: A school newsletter is a useful way of collecting and presenting information to keep staff, students and the community aware of local news and planned activities. It can be produced monthly or quarterly.

Use the information below and the Making a Living process skills (investigating, planning and designing, making or producing, marketing or using, evaluating) to develop a unit of work for producing a school newsletter.

Materials

- paper
- pictures
- posters/charts
- glue
- markers

Equipment

printing machine (photocopier, ink duplicator) if available

typewriter/computer

stapler for binding

Procedures

1. Plan the layout of the newsletter and identify different people for specific tasks.
2. Collect information and write stories/articles.
3. Teacher checks material for correction before typing or writing on paper.
4. Layout and print.
5. Collate for binding and distribution.
6. Distribute copies to each class for reading and ask for comment for future improvements.
7. If printing equipment not available, prepare news on a chart and display on school noticeboards for reading.

SUB-STRAND 3 Community projects

Main ideas

The main idea of the 'community projects' sub-strand is for students to use knowledge of their community's needs to initiate specific community improvement projects using the Making a Living process (investigate, plan and design, make or produce, market or use, evaluate). Projects can be in various fields including income-generation, health, culture, education, law and order, housing or environmental issues.

The learning outcomes for each upper primary grade for 'community projects' are shown in the following table:

Grade 6	Grade 7	Grade 8
6.3.3 Participate in projects to meet identified needs and opportunities for improvement within the school.	7.3.3 Initiate and plan cooperative projects that encourage community and school participation.	8.3.3 Plan and undertake an enterprising project to enable them to make a living.

Key words

projects, enterprise, opportunities, improvements, ownership, teamwork, self-reliance, creativity, handcrafts, action plan, marketing, donors, sustainability

Possible assessment tasks

Assessment aims to gather information on how well students achieve the learning outcomes for Sub-strand 3 (Community Projects). Clear criteria should be set for satisfactory completion of tasks.

The suggested activities are organised from simple school- or home-based activities (Grade 6 level) to more complex community-based ones (Grade 8 level); however, these levels are not prescriptive and teachers should choose activities according to students' needs and abilities.

Activities suitable for developing into assessment tasks include:

1. repair water pipes, wells, tanks, taps, gutters, drains
2. create and maintain footpaths, maintain roads and car parks
3. construct and maintain bus shelters, buildings, furniture, household equipment, bridges, roofs, steps, sea walls, noticeboards, haus win, rest houses, guest houses
4. create recreational areas, playground equipment, cooking areas, seats or shelters; plant shade trees; cut lawns; establish community musical bands
5. work with community handcraft groups to do weaving, sewing, carving, making cane furniture
6. offer education on financial management, literacy, setting up a small business, getting loans
7. give talks on health, immunisation, family planning, HIV/AIDS, good nutrition
8. conduct environmental projects and clean-up campaigns, plant trees, create flower gardens, establish plant nurseries, make hedges, establish protected areas in wildlife areas or coral reefs
9. become involved in catering and hospitality; be a tour guide, planning activities such as sightseeing, diving, surfing, trekking, mountain climbing
10. set up community agricultural projects for cash crops; food crops; vanilla, cocoa, coconut, oil palm crops; livestock (poultry, pigs, cattle); fishing
11. establish walkabout sawmill projects, based on sustainable logging, cutting of only matured and selected wood rather than natural forest.

Major links to other subjects

The 'community projects' sub-strand builds upon student learning in the lower primary subject Community Living. At the upper primary level, 'community projects' has major links to the substrand 'societies and communities' of Social Science, the substrand 'community health' of Personal Development and the substrand 'accuracy and error' of Mathematics. These links are noted as icons in the student books.

Teacher information

Identifying needs

Teachers need to review their school's needs and how these needs can best be translated into class projects. From the ideas listed below, the teacher can then decide on a topic that is most appropriate to undertake, taking into account students' prior knowledge as well as the resources and expertise available. These needs could include:

- The school's drinking and cooking water supply. Possible projects:
  - reviewing the school's water supply
  - assessing how effective it is in meeting the water needs of the school.
  - how water is collected (that is, from water supply board, water well, creeks, tanks)
  - what measures are in place to ensure the water is free from pollution
  - what needs to be in place to make better use of the water supply (for example, new tanks, pipes, taps)
- The school's canteen service. Possible projects:
  - using produce from school gardens in preparing food for sale
  - planning nutritious menus
  - running a school canteen
- The school buildings. Possible projects:
  - the need for safe shelters and a healthy environment for students, including well-maintained school furniture, buildings
  - what improvements could be made to the school grounds, such as pathways and flowerbeds

The importance of teamwork

Every day in our lives we associate with others in various relationships. We adopt various roles and responsibilities within the relationships in which we are involved. We need to develop certain skills for our relationships to grow as positive ones. During most of a school day students spend time in groups, and teamwork is very important if groups are to function effectively. To ensure students work as a team on class projects the following social skills need to be evident:

- communication
- decision-making
- listening
- cooperation
- developing trust and self-esteem
- being considerate
- honesty

Roles within a team could include:

Team leader—focuses attention on the task. This group member is aware of the goal of the group and actively seeks to direct and coordinate the task at hand.

Creative thinker—suggests a variety of possible solutions when faced with a problem situation. This type of person enjoys the prospect of challenging situations and is able to discover alternatives to solve problems.

Scribe—records details of the conversations and interactions of the group.

Collector—listens to group members and locates all the tools and materials required to complete a task.

Time keeper—ensures the team keeps to time schedules as well as cost schedules.

A team is successful when everyone in the team contributes to the success of a project, sharing the duties, and when team members resolve all conflicts within the team by looking at what is happening in the group to cause the conflict or problem and then collaboratively deciding what can be done to resolve the issue. Teams should also be aware of the need for capacity building—they need to understand the roles of community groups and NGOs and work with these groups in a partnership relationship.

Initiate and plan cooperative projects

Once a school's or community's needs are identified and prioritised, planning is required to get the project started. The following points should be considered before any serious planning occurs:

- Brainstorm ideas on how to generate plans and proposals. This can mean walking around the school or community and collecting data, information, sketches, cost estimates, and materials and tools needed if a plan is to be developed.
- Consider possible options and identify priorities and constraints. This could mean prioritising identified needs and problems and deciding which project to carry out based on urgency, benefit and potential to encourage community participation and gender equity.
- Consider what appropriate resources and equipment is available, including the skilled and talented persons in the community, the type of natural resources and the tools and equipment that can be used for specific projects.
- Formulate the criteria that will be used to assess the project.

To prepare a project action plan

When planning a project, an action plan has to be made. Planning is matching together activities, time and resources. When planning, ask the following type of questions:

- ➢ What has to be done?
- ➢ How is it to be done?
- ➢ What is needed?
- ➢ Who will do it?
- ➢ When is it to be done?
- ➢ How long will it take?

A good planner can identify the likely problems that could occur during the project and plan to prevent them happening. To prepare a project action plan:

- Make a list of activities.
- Place them in the order that they should occur.
- Estimate how long each activity should take.
- Decide whether more than one activity can be undertaken at the same time.

Possible cooperative projects

Teachers need to decide on which cooperative projects are the most appropriate to develop, taking into account students' prior knowledge as well as the resources and expertise available. These projects may include:

- cooperative projects within the school or local community, such as building a haus win, public noticeboard or plant nursery, road maintenance, water supply, environmental projects
- community-driven initiatives that promote self-reliance, self-esteem and ownership and encourage community participation, such as village or town clean up, market clean up, beach clean up or community hall building (for example, church, haus man, haus meri, haus tambaran)
- work with partner organisations—government departments such as Department of Primary Industry (DPI); health extension officers; local level councils; NGOs; CBOs.

Principles of planning and running an enterprise project

Apart from community projects to improve the community's quality of life, other group projects could be undertaken to generate income. This requires preparing a business plan for the proposed business. In preparing a business plan the group must decide:

- how the business will be set up
- the cost of setting up a business
- how long it will take to set up the business
- what will be sold

A business plan is an estimate of the future sales, costs and profits that can be achieved. It consists of a *sales plan* and an *expenditure plan.*

Project resources estimate

To carry out any project, human, material and equipment resources will be required. Information can be obtained from the project plan to assist in preparing a list of resources. Surveying the required resources can be done with the help of a Project Resources Form.

Project Resources Form

Project activity	Required human resources —number, skills and knowledge	Required equipment	Required materials

Steps to fill the project resources form:

1 Identify all the project activities. List these in column 1 of the form.

2 Examine each of the activities in turn and imagine how that activity will be performed. Ask: who is going to perform the activity? Will they require special skills or knowledge? Make a list in column 2 of the numbers and skills of all human resources required.

3 For each activity decide if equipment will be required. The equipment might be bought, rented or borrowed. Enter the information in column 3.

4 Examine the activities and decide what materials will be required. Enter the information in column 4.

Project cost estimate

A project cost estimate will have to be prepared to determine the amount of money required to finance the project. Expenditure can be grouped under five headings and their costs determined as follows:

- ➢ labour costs
- ➢ materials
- ➢ equipment
- ➢ transportation and accommodation
- ➢ miscellaneous

An expenditure form similar to the project resources form should be devised so that costs can be estimated and recorded. Expenditure in each area can be estimated using a similar process (for example, a transportation requirements form can be drawn up and used to identify all the transportation requirements).

A decision will have to be made on how to finance a project. There are three possible sources of funds:

Self-help—There are many forms of self-help. Each has in common that the group provides all or part of the necessary funds or resources. These can be obtained by fund-raising, selling unwanted items, contributing gifts and so on.

Loans—These can be obtained from private individuals, organisations or banks. A loan is money borrowed for an agreed period of time and it is always paid back with interest. A loan is only appropriate when the project will make enough money to repay the debt.

Grants—Unlike loans, grants do not have to be repaid. They are given to finance specific project requirements. The money must not be used by the group to fund activities that were not approved by the agency that gave the grant. The three main sources of grants are local individuals or organisations, national organisations and international organisations.

Basic bookkeeping and records

Bookkeeping or accounting is the process of keeping a record of details every time money is spent or received. It is the responsibility of the group's treasurer to keep a record of all financial transactions. The treasurer must be able both to show and to prove what has happened to the group's money. So the treasurer needs to keep not only records but also:

- receipts—a written form as proof of cash payment
- bills—given out when a cash purchase is made. A bill is also made out when payment is required for a credit transaction
- invoice—given out when a credit transaction is undertaken (for example, purchases made or work performed with payment to be made at a later date)

Invoices, bills and receipts are the proof of transactions.

Accounts are kept in order to keep a record of all financial transactions. There are many different ways of recording this information, but whichever method is chosen, be sure to be *consistent*. The same rules for recording the information must be used every time. Accounts need to be able to be checked to ensure they are correct.

Project management skills

During the project the group will need to use management skills. This will include using the project plan and budget to determine whether the project is proceeding as planned. This means that all issues related to financial control, quality control, planned procurement of materials and equipment and time management need to be monitored by the project manager to ensure conflicts, if they arise, are dealt with quickly before they cause a problem.

Legal requirements for setting up a business enterprise

There are many government procedures for setting up a business in Papua New Guinea. These include:

- registration of a business
- understanding labour laws and employee entitlements
- taxation paid by a business

Teachers should write to the relevant bodies to gain further information when undertaking a business enterprise.

Class projects

School improvements projects

Choose projects from the list below that are appropriate for the school's local area and available resources. Set clear criteria for the satisfactory completion of tasks.

1. Footpaths. Make new pathways leading to classrooms and other school buildings. Maintain existing pathways. Concrete the paths. Line river stone or used tyres along the footpaths.

2. Tree planting. Plant shade or fruit trees in the school. Plant trees around the perimeters of the school to mark out school boundaries.

3. Maintenance of buildings. Carry out minor maintenance and improvement works on school buildings, such as wall painting, chalkboard painting, replacing broken and rusty roofing iron and gutters, and repairing broken steps or classroom furniture (desks, tables etc.).

4. Flower gardening. Make flower gardens as a school beautification activity around classrooms, school offices, school flag raising area.

Making or producing enterprise projects

1. Agricultural projects—chicken poultry; piggery; raising cattle; growing crops; growing commercial crops such as vanilla, cocoa, coconut, oil palm; fishing

2. Handcraft projects—carvings, masks, artefacts such as bilums, woven baskets

3. Catering and hospitality projects—tour guide, guest house, sightseeing, diving, surfing and other tourism activities

4. Ecotourism projects—showing preservation sites as tourist attractions, botanical gardens, wildlife areas, coral reefs, Kokoda trail trekking, mountain climbing

5. Walkabout sawmill projects—allowing for sustainable logging, cutting only matured and selected wood rather than destroying natural forest through large logging activity

Additional Material: Projects and Investigations

Managing resources (Year 6)

1. Vegetable garden

Select an area in your school for a garden. Select local vegetables like aibika, chinese cabbage, round cabbage, cucumber, tomato, pumpkin, beans, egg-plant and capsicum. Sell your produce at the local market or to teachers at the school.

2. Raising chickens

Build a small kunai or sago-roof house with one room. Ask parents to donate local chickens to the school for their children's agriculture lesson. The birds should be looked after and housed properly. Feed them with local food. Sell eggs to staff and students.

3. Raising pigs

Build a small kunai or sago-roof house with two to three strong rooms. Ask parents to donate local pigs to the school for their children's agriculture lesson. The animals should be cared for and housed properly. Feed them with local food and sell the pigs at the age of nine to ten months. Pigs should be sold before the end of the school academic year.

4. Building a fish pond

Select a running creek near your school and change it into a fish pond. Make a fence around it and put in some fresh water fish. The best local fresh water fish would be: tilapia, golden carp and cold fish. Sell the fish to your teachers and parents.

5. Orchid nursery

Select an empty space in your school for an orchid garden. Collect local orchids from the village and plant them in your garden. When established, take cuttings and sell them to local people or visitors to your school.

6. Shellfish farming

Select a shallow sea water area near a reef or in a lagoon. Fence an area measuring 4 ¥ 4 metres using mangrove poles. Tie the poles with wire or cane ropes. Next place your shellfish inside. Harvest them after six months and sell them at the local market in your area.

7. Cut flower arrangements and flower leis

Consider planning a project to sell cut flower arrangements or flower leis. Create gardens of flowering plants. Plant flowering trees in your school grounds too.

8. Compost

Set up an area for a compost heap. Collect organic matter. Use the compost to enrich the gardens.

Managing Resources (Years 7 and 8)

1. Rainfall

- Using the library, read about the rainfall patterns of other provinces.
- Class discuss why Gulf, Western and Baimuru received a lot of rainfall throughout the year.
- Students draw the rainfall pattern for their province.

2. Soil and compost

- Students examine the topsoil in their garden plots. List in their books what they saw.
- Class construct a compost heap for their plots.
- Using the library, students study the nitrogen cycle and draw the diagram in their books.

3. Humidity

- Using the library, students read about humidity and which plants grow best in this weather condition.
- Study the map of Papua New Guinea and calculate the average humidity of your province.
- Why are farmers so concerned about plant humidity?

4. Planting in Enga

- Students locate Enga on the map and suggest what sorts of plants would best grow there.
- Make a list of vegetables that would grow successfully in Enga.
- Discuss the vegetable and livestock production options for Engan farmers.

5. Vegetable crops

- Students list root vegetables and estimate their maturity dates. They can check these dates with parents and elders in the community.
- Class discuss from the list in activity 4 above, which vegetable crop has low estimate returns. Why?
- Why is there more demand for sweet potatoes in the highland provinces than there is for taro?
- Class discuss the types of crops that are classified under the vegetable group.
- Students group these vegetables under – root vegetables, leaf vegetables and fruit vegetables. Teacher can remind the class that vegetables are short-term crops.
- Teacher and students can explore the advantages of growing vegetables.

6. Economic importance of crops and animals

- Students and teacher discuss the economical importance of crops and animals in their region and how these influence the traditional culture of the society.

7. Your school garden

- Students go out to the school garden and select a good site for a vegetable garden.
- Discuss reasons for harvesting vegetables at the right time for sale.
- Students practise good garden management in their small vegetable plots.
- Teacher shows how to transplant seedlings from nursery beds to the garden.
- Class investigates the best organic materials for mulching the garden.

8. Selling vegetables at the market

- Class finds out the different prices of vegetables sold at the market.
- Ask local women to show how to bundle the different vegetables sold at market.
- The class carries out a market survey. Find out about price, demand for certain vegetables and whether the goods sold at the market consisted of three main food groups (energy, protein and carbohydrates).

9. Seeds and seedlings

- Discuss ways to collect local seeds and preserve them for your gardens.
- Which seeds did not germinate in the nursery boxes?
- Which insects destroyed the seedlings in the nursery? How can you control them?

Better Living (Year 6)

1. Belts, necklaces, arm and ankle bands

Gather resources and learn the skills to make belts, necklaces, arm and ankle bands to sell. Make imaginative use of local materials for a truly Papua New Guinean look.

2. Brooms and rakes

Investigate the need for new brooms and rakes in your community. If there is a need, make strong, attractive brooms and rakes from available resources. Determine an affordable price.

3. Clothes repair service

Plan a clothes repair service for children or adults. Consider charges according to the size of damage and materials and time required.

4. Gardening service

Establish a service to weed gardens, rake up leaves, trim hedges and beautify flower gardens. Determine an hourly rate per person and seek customers.

5. Hats

Plan a range of designs for hats for both males and females. They can be made from fabric or from local materials.

6. Kitchen utensils

Consider which kitchen utensils could be made from local or recycled materials. Items could be graters, spoons, knives, chopping boards, soap holders, pot stands or tongs. Make them simple, useful and attractive.

7. Learn to read and write

Explore whether there are people who would like to learn to read and write. Cater for individual or group interests. Calculate a reasonable cost for each hour of teaching.

8. Plant cuttings

Investigate whether people would be prepared to buy plant cuttings. Take cuttings from plants in the garden. Sell in bundles for one or two kina a bundle.

9. Reading materials

Collect old newspapers, magazines or books. Look in second-hand shops for books that could be re-sold. Advertise reading materials for sale at reasonable prices.

10. Removal service

Offer to provide quotes for removal services – no job too big or too small. It could be rubbish or furniture removal. Calculate a reasonable cost according to the number of people and the time needed to do a job.

11. School lunches

Plan a variety of foods that could be sold to children on different days. You could sell ice blocks, fruit drinks, hard-boiled eggs, sausages on sticks, sandwiches, doughnuts, peanut toffee, chips, soup or fruit. Sell at affordable prices.

12. Special food for special events

Develop skills to make iced cakes or attractive finger-food for special celebrations. Let others know that you can provide special food for special events.

13. Vases

Design a range of attractive vases or plant holders made from different local materials such as bamboo, coconut shell, clay, recycled plastic or glass containers, tyres or bush timber. Sell at markets, open days or parent gatherings.

Better living (Years 7 and 8)

1. Class cookhouse

Create different designs for a class cookhouse that is possible to build with resources available. Choose one design, develop a plan of action with a time-line. Implement the plan.

2. Class shopping centre

Set up a class shopping centre. As a seller, role-play how to promote the products you sell and how to give friendly service to customers. As a shopper, role-play how to be a wise consumer.

3. Craft book

Write a project sheet for a craft idea from everyone in the class. Include a diagram or photograph and instructions. Select the most suitable ideas and make them into a book that can be photocopied, bound and sold.

4. Do-it-yourself maintenance jobs

Identify repair and maintenance jobs that can be done as class projects in your classroom, school or community. Advertise your services to others, at reasonable prices.

5. Improvised cooking utensils and equipment

Be creative in designing and making cooking utensils and equipment from local materials and by recycling available resources.

6. One-pot cookbook

Create recipes for balanced meals that are cooked in one container, for example, a meal in a coconut shell, stuffed pumpkin, sweet potato or pawpaw, fried rice or bamboo tube meals.

7. Preserving

Preserve food using different methods. Make jam, pickles, smoked fish, frozen fruit juice as ice-blocks or dried fruit slices.

8. Screen-printing

Set up a T-shirt screen-printing service. Advertise your designs at affordable prices.

9. Target a tourist

Observe buying habits of tourists. List things that you could make to appeal to a tourist from overseas. Design and make something to sell. (Local people could buy it too, but design it for a tourist.)

10. Toys

Design, make and sell a toy or gift for a child. Identify the qualities that make it safe and appealing.

11. Campaign for a clean environment

Identify unsatisfactory rubbish disposal practices in your locality. Plan and implement a campaign to keep your community beautiful.

12. Catering service

Plan to cater for functions such as parent or teacher meetings, birthdays or other special events. Estimate the cost per person. Design menus in different price ranges. What could you provide for K2.00 a person? K5.00 a person? Or K10.00 a person?

13. Food stall

Create realistic plans for a school canteen or food stall. Choose the site, collect building materials, construct and evaluate.

14. Food to sell

Plan a range of foods to sell throughout a year, considering food availability at different times of the year. Include fresh fruit, drinks, ice-blocks, ice cream, sandwiches, salads and cooked food.

15. Furniture making

Create designs for furniture items that could be made from new or recycled materials in your community. Make and sell a variety of furniture items. Evaluate designs and consider ways by which they could be improved.

16. Jam or pickles

Make jam or pickles from local fruit or vegetables. Build up a collection of clean glass jars or buy cheap drinking glasses. Design labels. Cover tops with a circular piece of cloth held on with a rubber band.

17. Maintenance of the community environment

Advertise services (voluntary labour or for a fee) to repair and maintain buildings or areas in the community environment (sports fields, roadsides, church gardens, market benches or bus stops).

18. Marketing

Design a distinctive logo, motto, brand, label or packaging for your 'class business'. Create a 'jingle-type' advertisement that can be sung over the radio. Plan how to market your products using advertising strategies.

19. Recipe book

Create and sell a recipe book with recipes for foods that are available in your locality.

20. Rising prices

List five common items that families buy on a regular basis. Record the brand and size of each item. Choose two shops. Once a month over a year, record the prices for these items. Discuss price variations and how this might affect family budgets.

21. Wise consumer habits

Plan and implement a project aimed at raising awareness of wise consumer habits.

Community Development (Year 6)

1. Community resource map

Draw a resource map of the community you live in. Then based on the resources map, plan and carry out a project to promote your communities resources. Suggestions: sell tapioca cake, establish a traditional craft shop or vanilla farm and so on.

2. Community water supply project

Your school community needs water tanks to supply clean drinking water to both teachers and students. Write a letter to your local ward councillor requesting financial help to establish two bushman water tanks in the school.

3. Drying fish – smoking method

Plan and build a small smoke-house in your community to dry fish.

4. Community Awareness campaign

Form small groups in your class and prepare charts, role-plays, write speeches, songs and poems to educate your community on current issues like HIV/AIDS, drug abuse, malnutrition and the importance of a clean living environment.

5. Classroom maintenance and repair

Your school has a lot of dirty and broken tables, chairs and bookshelves. They needed repair. How can you fix them?

6. Maintaining rusting roofing iron

Your classroom's roofing irons are rusting away. You need to prevent rusting. What can you do? Make a list of tools and materials required and write out a plan of action.

7. Collecting good, clean rain water

It usually rains heavily and you wish to collect rain water. But you do not have a gutter connected to your roofing iron for rain water to run through. What other bush materials could you use instead of a gutter and water tank? How would you collect rain water?

8. Building a small bridge over a creek

You have a small creek that runs through your village community or school. Sketch a plan for a bridge. Collect all materials needed to build the bridge over the creek.

9. School sign board

Your shool does not have a sign board. Draw up a plan for your sign board and collect all the materials and tools needed. Build a school sign board.

10. Design a community game

- Make a board game with 40 squares – each square numbered from 1 (start) to 40 (finish).
- Write five messages that benefit a community.
  Example: PMV bus service is always on time
- Write five messages that don't benefit the community.
  Example: Rubbish is dumped in the river
- Write your ten messages on random squares.
- Write instructions on how to play the game, then play the game with your friend.

Community development (Years 7 and 8)

1. Clothes line

Design a clothes line to hang and dry your wet clothes after laundry. Plant two posts not more than 6 m apart. Nail a 'T' cross on top of each post. Tie strong rope or wire rope from one post to the other post. Leave space between the ropes for drying.

2. Classroom news board

Use a piece of thin plywood (1 m x 1 m) or empty cartons as a class news board. Divide the spaces into sections: World news, National news, Local news, or Health, Sports, Social news. News can be collected from newspapers and magazines and displayed weekly.

3. Rubbish-drum stand

Design a rubbish-drum stand for standing the rubbish drum close to the road near your house. A stand makes it easier for the rubbish collection workers to lift the drum and dump rubbish onto their rubbish collection truck or tractor for disposal.

4. Market food display shelves

At markets in rural communities in PNG, food and items for sale are most often displayed on the ground. It is unhygienic. Collect bamboo, strong pitpits, bush timber, palm barks and ropes from the bush to build market display shelves at waist height.

5. Building stalls and shelters and stages

Building stalls to sell food, shelters for shade and stages for speakers and guests at community gatherings, school open days and carnivals. These rough shelters can be built from bush materials such as bamboo, bush timber, bush ropes, coconut leaves, kunai grass and other leaves and bush materials. Design, plan and build shelters.

6. Community or school 'cleanathon'

Make people aware of the importance of living in a clean and healthy environment. Work with your village elders, local councillor, head teacher and teachers to organise a clean-up day. Make fences around the village or school. Clean village cemeteries, community halls, church buildings, beaches and market areas.

7. School bell or church bell

Your present school bell does not give a loud sound. Many students come late to school. What materials would you collect to make a bell?

8. Cassava or tapioca scraper

Tapioca cakes are a favourite food to eat at home. They are also sold in markets. Make a cassava scraper. It can also be used for scraping banana. Collect a thin sheet of metal (30 cm x 40 cm). Nail strips of timber under the edges. Make a handle at one end. Use a hammer and nail to make many little holes on the metal sheet. The rough surface is used for scraping.

9. Tyre plant pot

Tyre plant pot is made from used tyres. Collect old used car tyres (small car tyres are an ideal size). Cut off the inner round edges using a very sharp knife. Press the back of the tyre inward while pulling the inner edges backward. Cut flat pieces from the rubber tube and sew and cover the bottom end using a string rope. (Sharpen one end of a wire and heat it in the fire until the end becomes red-hot. Make holes through the tyre for sewing). Fill the tyre with soil and plant your desired plant. Paint designs. It can be sold for money.

10. Weaving mats

Mats are useful to sit on, sleep on and for serving food. The types and styles of weaving mats vary from region to region in PNG. Materials used for weaving mats are pandanus leaves, coconut leaves, oil palm leaves and water straws. Invite a skilled person from the local community to the school to demonstrate making mats. Students can weave mats. These could be sold in the market for money.

Forms

It is important for students to recognise and be able to fill in relevant forms that will help with everyday living such as opening a bank account, filling in a bank loan application, applying for a post box or applying for telephone connection.

There are also governmental forms such as Statuary Declaration forms, taxation forms, leave application forms, and business registration forms that students need to be able to fill in when required.

Most of these forms can be obtained from relevant government offices, post offices and banks.

Some forms are included here. Teachers can photocopy these forms and let students practice filling them in. Alternatively, teachers can collect relevant forms for student to fill in.

PAPUA NEW GUINEA

STATUTORY DECLARATION

I, (a) *of*

do solemnly and sincerely declare that ***(b)***

And I make this solemn declaration by virtue of the Oaths, Affirmations and Statutory Declarations Act 1962 conscientiously believing the statements contained therein to be true in every particular.

Declared at *(c)* ....

the *day of* , **2004** ***Before me –***

(d) ....

(e) ....

(a) Here insert name, address and occupation of person making the declaration.
(b) Here insert the matter declared to. Where the matter is long, it should be set out in numbered paragraphs.
(c) Signature of person making the declaration.
(d) Signature of person before whom the declaration is made.
(e) Here insert title of person before whom the declaration is made.

Note: *Any person who wilfully makes a false statement in a Statutory Declaration is guilty of an indictable offence, and is liable of imprisonment, with or without hard labour, for four years.*

Statement of Position

Liabilities (What you owe)

Home Loan from ____________ K ______

Other Loans - Name of Lender & Account No.

______ ______ K ______

______ ______ K ______

______ ______ K ______

Rates, Taxes, Store Accounts etc.

____________ K ______

____________ K ______

____________ K ______

All Other Debts & Liabilities

____________ K ______

____________ K ______

____________ K ______

Total Liabilities K ______

Budget - Monthly Payments

Home Loans K ______

Other Loans K ______

Motor Vehicle Running Costs K ______

Rent K ______

Electricity & Phone K ______

Insurance, Rates & Taxes K ______

School Fees K ______

Wantoks K ______

General Living Expenses K ______

Total Payments per month K ______

Assets (What you own)

Value of Home ____________ K ______

Address: Lot ______ Sect ______ Suburb ______

Motor Vehicle ____________ K ______

Accounts - Bank ______ Branch ______

______ ______ K ______

______ ______ K ______

______ ______ K ______

______ ______ K ______

Furniture K ______

Other Assets Description (if a property, advise type of residence, village or lot, sect and suburb)

____________ K ______

____________ K ______

____________ K ______

____________ K ______

____________ K ______

Total Assets: K ______

Monthly Income (Attach 3 payslips, financial statements)

Applicants monthly **net** income K ______

Other monthly income - give details

____________ K ______

____________ K ______

____________ K ______

____________ K ______

Total Income per month K ______

I have read and understood the information contained herein. The details completed are a true and accurate record given to enable the Bank to assess my/our loan request.

Applicant's Signature ______ Date ______

Applicant's Signature ______ Date ______

Bank Use Only

☐ Approved in principle - Proceed to Loan Contract/Security.

☐ Declined-advise customer.

Date ______

Loan Application for Individuals

Bank South Pacific

For housing, personal and school fee loans.

Bank South Pacific

"OUR BANK"

BSP 11/02 087

Hints to help you complete this form

To enable prompt consideration of your loan application please ensure the following has been attended to or provided:-

- Loan application has been completed in full both front and back.
- Latest 3 payslips are enclosed with your application.
- Letter of confirmation of employment from your employer.
- Quotation or invoices for the purpose of the loan.
- For school fee loans please provide school bank deposit form, or an invoice from the school(s).

For assistance in completing this form contact your nearest Bank South Pacific branch.

Bank South Pacific
"OUR BANK"

Please complete all pages neatly by hand and send/deliver to any branch of Bank South Pacific

Purchase Price: K ______ Own Contribution: K ______ Loan Requested: K ______

Purpose ______ Monthly/Fortnightly payment offered: K ______

Your Personal Details

Surname ______ Given Name(s) ______

Date of Birth ______ Marital Status ______ Ages of Dependents ______

Full name of your partner ______ Date of Birth ______

Your residential address ______

Date you moved there ______ Home Phone No ______

Who owns this residence? ☐ Self (provide rate notice) ☐ Relatives ☐ *Landlord - give details

*Landlord/Agent's Name ______ Phone No ______

Postal Address ______

Your previous address ______

Years/Months at this address ______

Name, address, phone number and relationship of nearest relative not living with you.

______

Credit History - Credit Reference: previous loans, finance companies, stores etc.

Name	Address	Account Number
(1)		
(2)		
(3)		

Have you ever been bankrupt or had any judgement or legal proceedings against you? ☐ Yes* ☐ No

*Details ______

Employment Details - Self

Occupation ______

Employer's Name ______

Employer's Address ______

Phone Number ______

Date Commenced ______

Previous Employer ______

Years There ______

Partner

Occupation ______

Employer's Name ______

Employer's Address ______

Phone Number ______

Date Commenced ______

Previous Employer ______

Years There ______

Bank South Pacific DEPOSIT SLIP

Date: ____ / ____ / ____

Lodged as per slip therewith

Branch

For
CREDIT

The Bank is not be responsible for delays in transmission

Proceeds of cheques etc. not to be available until collected

Amount **K**

Teller and Bank Stamp

Bank South Pacific

DEPOSIT SLIP

Branch: ____________________ Date: ____ / ____ / ____

The Bank is not responsible for delays in transmission

Proceeds of cheques etc. not to be available until collected

Drawer	**Bank**	**Branch**	**Cash**	

Teller	No. of Items	Paid in By (Signature & Address)	Tfr. Fee	Cheques as per Reverse

For **CREDIT** of	BSP No.	Account No.	T.C.	**K**

461-595 (05/02)

STEPHENS Printing 554-10-03

Bank of South Pacific Limited

WITHDRAWAL

Branch No.	Account No.	Date
Branch Name	Customer Name	
Amount in Words		

Teller **Bank Use** Final PB Balance **K**	Signature(s)	**K**

474 - 564 (06/02)

STEPHENS Printing

Glossary

abundance	plenty, more than enough
adapt	to change and become suited to something new
aesthetic	artistic, beautiful
aibika	a common green vegetable in Papua New Guinea, good for boiling with chicken or pork to make soup
alternative	instead of something else, like a crop planted instead of another crop
amenities	things that are pleasant or useful in a house or a community
ancestors	a relation who lived long ago
appropriate	suitable, a proper way of doing things
bacteria	tiny living things, that sometimes cause disease
bake	to cook food in an oven, or an enclosed space where the heat is dry
balanced meal	a meal that is good for you because it has some food from each of the food groups
bank statement	a record from the bank showing details of money in an account
barter	a trading system where you exchange goods without using money
bilas	decoration
biodiversity	the variety of plants and animals in an environment
blend	to mix together
boil	to cook food in very hot bubbling liquid
botanical	relating to plants or the study of plants
broadcast	a radio or television program
budget	a plan to spend money
carbohydrate	the main source of energy in food, found in food such as yams, sago and potatoes
care	to look after the well-being of someone or something
caterpillar	a small crawling creature that eats plants and turns into a butterfly or moth
ceremony	a special event to celebrate something, such as a yam harvest
chemical fertilizer	fertilizers made in a factory
clam	a large shellfish, with white and grey flesh
commercial agriculture	farming animals or crops on a large scale for cash
communication	passing news or messages from one person to another
community	a group of people living in the same locality who share something in common
conservation	protecting the environment
conserve	to use something wisely so it will not run out, or be damaged
consumable	anything that can be used
consumer	someone who buys or uses something
consumerism	the belief that it is good for a person or a community to use large amounts of goods and services
consumption	eating or using up something
contamination	to make something dirty or impure
contour	a line on a map which joins points that are at the same height above sea level
cover crop	a crop in which other plants or animals live
criteria	the standard by which you judge something
crotalaria	a legume plant – otherwise known as botol plauwa in Tok Pisin
culture	the customs, traditions and beliefs that make up our way of life
deforestation	cutting down trees in a forest. The opposite of reforestation
democratic	a belief that everyone has equal rights
demonstrate	to show how something is done
destruction	when something is destroyed or ruined

disease	illness or sickness
disposal	throwing something away
dispute	a disagreement or argument
disturb	to interrupt something or someone
diversity	many different kinds of something
domesticated animals	animals that are tamed and looked after by people
dysentery	an infection that causes diarrhoea
ecology	the relation of living creatures to each other and to their environment
economical	not wasteful, good value
ecosystem	a community of plants or animals that are connected by where or how they live
element	an important part of something
enterprise	a business such as farming or running a shop
environment	the world around us, and the conditions that affect growth and development
equipment	the things you need to do something
essential	the most important things, which we cannot do without
evaluate	to decide the value of something
expenditure	spending or payments
exploit	to use something, often to use something selfishly, so that it destroys other things or a way of life
exploration	discovery
export	to sell something overseas, like gas, gold or coffee, to earn money for our country
faeces	solid waste from the bowels of animals or humans
fats	greasy or oily nutrients in food which are a source of energy
fauna	the animals in an area
finance	to do with money
financial record	a record of money spent and earned
fingerlings	tiny young fish
flammable	something that can easily go on fire
food groups	the main types of food that supply us with protein, carbohydrates, fats, vitamins, minerals
fry	to cook something in a pan with oil or fat
furniture	tables, chairs, cupboards, beds and other moveable things we have in our houses or schools
galip	a type of nut, or the tree it comes from
generate	to create something or make something happen
geology	the study of the Earth and rocks
grill	to cook food by heat given off from very hot coals or a hot cooker
habitat	the place where an animal or a plant lives naturally
harvest	to gather and save a crop from the garden or farm; the crops that is gathered
healthy	in good condition, free from sickness
hectare	a unit of measurement equal to 10,000 square metres
heritage	the values and customs passed down to us from our ancestors
hygiene	cleanliness
improvise	to make or do something using whatever is available
income	money that you are paid for doing a job
influence	to have an effect on someone or something
innovation	a new way of doing something
integrated farming	to combine different activities to improve the farm
interdependent	when things depend on each other
interview	to ask questions and collect information
investigate	to find out more about something
invoice	a bill for money that is to be paid to someone for something
irrigation	to supply water to crops through pipes or channels
kangkong	a type of green vegetable used to flavour food

kumu	a name for green leaves that you can eat
kwashiorkor	a form of malnutrition caused by not enough protein in the diet
labour	the work someone does
landmark	something you can easily see from a distance, sometimes marking a boundary
landscaping	laying out a garden to a set plan
laulau	a soft fruit that you can eat
laundry	the job of washing and ironing clothes
lawn	an area of short grass, near a house
legume	a plant that has seeds in long pods. Peas and beans are legumes
leisure	free time
leucaena	a legume plant – otherwise known as marmar in Tok Pisin
lifestyle	the way people live their lives
livelihood	the way in which you earn a living
louvers	slats of glass, wood or metal, in windows
maintenance	to repair or keep things in good condition
making a living	the things we do to earn money to help us live well
malaria	a dangerous disease, spread by mosquitoes, that causes fever and shivering
malnutrition	weakness caused by not having enough food
mammals	humans and animals who feed their young with their mothers' milk
management	a planned way to do something
mangrove	a tree that grows in salt water
manipulate	to handle something skilfully
manure	animal dung used for fertilizing the garden
marasmus	a form of malnutrition caused by not enough carbohydrate in the diet
market	a place where things are bought and sold
media	newspapers, radio, television
minerals	things like iron and calcium, found in food, which help keep us healthy
mixed cropping	when more than one type is planted in a garden
modern	whatever is happening today, the latest ideas or fashions
modify	to change something
mulch	natural material placed around a plant to protect it
nutrients	substances in food, like protein, carbohydrate, fats, vitamins, minerals and water, that you need to keep healthy
nutrition	food that helps keep us healthy
organic farming	growing crops with the use of natural fertilizers, such as manure
organism	any living plant or animal
partnership	two people or two groups who work together
pau	a type of nut that hangs in bunches
perishable	something that is likely to rot quickly, like fruit or vegetables
permaculture	'permanent agriculture', to encourage self-sufficiency and sustainable living by growing a mix of plants which last for a long time, and farming plants and animals together
pesticide	poison used to kill insects and pests
pests	destructive or annoying insects or animals, like cockroaches or rats
photosynthesis	the way by which green plants use sunlight to turn carbon dioxide and water into food and oxygen
pickling	preserving vegetables in vinegar
plan	a way to do something, like a diagram
poison	something that can kill or harm you
pollution	anything that makes air, water or soil dirty
population	the number of people or plants in an area
preserve	to protect something or keep it in good condition
procreria	a legume plant

produce	make, create
productivity	the way in which a lot of things can be produced
profit	money left over after expenses or costs have been paid
project	a plan to make something
propagate	to reproduce new plants using parts of existing plants
protein	things in food that help us to grow well
puereria	a legume plant – otherwise known as rop plauwa in Tok Pisin
pylons	the towers that support electric power lines
pyrethrum	a plant grown, especially in the Highlands, to make pesticide
quarantine	keeping people or animals away from others to prevent a disease from spreading
questionnaire	a list of questions to gather information
receipt	a written proof of a payment that has been made
recycle	to reuse something well, instead of throwing it away
reforestation	planting new trees in an area where there used to be forest. This helps prevent soil erosion
resistant	hard to break, hard to get through
resources	anything that can be used to create wealth, or make life better
revenue	income or money that comes into our country, or to our school, or village
rotation	changing the crops that are planted, each planting season
rural	to do with villages or country areas, not towns or cities
safety	the way in which we protect someone or something from danger
sanitation	the way in which places are kept clean
sediment	the soil that is carried away by a river, especially in a flood
self-reliance	able to do or decide things for yourself without relying on others
species	a group of animals or plants that are very similar
staple food	the main food eaten by people, e.g. sago, sweet potato, taro, yams, rice
statistics	information given in figures
subsistence farming	growing only enough to live on, not to sell
sustainable	to support something and keep it going
symptom	the sign of being healthy or unhealthy
technology	a system where machines or tools are used to make something easier
terracing	a series of flat areas of ground, like steps cut into a hill, used for growing rice for example
tools	things we use to get something done, or fix something
traditional	ways of the past, old ways of doing things that have not changed for hundreds of years
traditional calendar	traditional crop calendar used by local people to plant and harvest crops
typhoid	sickness caused by water polluted by human faeces
unemployed	not working in a paid job
unenclosed	not having a fence or wall around it
urban	to do with the towns, not the villages or rural areas
vegetation	plants in general
ventilation	ways to provide a room with fresh air
viable	successful
virgin forest	a forest that has not been touched or spoiled by cutting down lots of trees
vitamins	important things in food that keep us healthy
warranty	a promise that something will be repaired or replaced if it is faulty
yield	the total amount of crops or profit produced